NIXON

NIXON

RALPH de TOLEDANO

HENRY HOLT AND COMPANY

NEW YORK

PREFACE

This is not an "authorized" biography. Any sins of commission
and emphasis are my own. Richard Nixon has cooperated only
to this extent: He has opened his files to me and answered the
questions I put to him. He has in no way influenced or attempted to influence this account. In preparing these pages,
therefore, I have relied on the verifiable record and, where I
was present, on direct reporting. Here and there, I suspect, are
passages and viewpoints to which Nixon will take exception.
This book has no imprimatur.

In the following chapters I have set out to place Richard
Nixon in the context of his times and of the issues which have
agitated the country. I have not tried to gather the small details of his life. This book will not tell you what Nixon eats
for breakfast. It will tell you that he reads Tolstoi, but not
that he has read and reread the lives of Robert LaFollette, of
Theodore Roosevelt and Woodrow Wilson. It will not tell
you that he was relaxing to the music of Tchaikovsky long
before the serious critics rediscovered it. It touches on his marriage and his home life only lightly. This book is fundamen-
tally an account of political struggle and political achievement.
In short, I have written about the Richard Nixon I have
known and covered since the early days of the Hiss Case.

I had originally planned to include two chapters in this
account. The first, "A Study in Method," would have been
an analysis of the systematic falsification of the Nixon record

by such publications as *The New Republic* and the New York *Post*. It would have included mention of Richard Rovere's armchair analysis of Nixon's character and personality—and the snide remarks about the nature of Nixon's Quaker faith— which he wrote for *Harper's* without so much as bothering to interview the subject. As a study in method, Rovere's piece of intellectual shoddy can be compared with the excellent reporting of Cabell Phillips in the New York *Times*. When Phillips was assigned to do an extended article on Nixon's campaign technique, he told Vic Johnson of the Republican Senatorial Campaign Committee:

"I think you should know, Vic, that I have a bad impression of Nixon, although I've never had an opportunity to know him before. But I'm going to try to do an objective job." After watching Nixon at work, Phillips told Johnson that his opinion had changed. His article, which appeared in the *Times* magazine, reflected that change. It was the work of an honest reporter—and it proved, incidentally, that those who hate Nixon most are those who know him least. In a chapter on the "method against Nixon," it would have been interesting to point out that the Phillips article was in print at the time Rovere did his clip-and-paste attempt at head-shrinking.

The second projected chapter would have been a listing of "Things People Say Nixon Said Which He Never Said"— "Truman's war" and "the party of treason" being but two. But it seemed to me that I would be arguing with myself and with some rather soiled phantoms.

The record of Nixon's life speaks for itself. He is an unusual phenomenon in American politics—not because of his amazing rise to pre-eminence, but because in that rise he was always his own man. Contrary to popular belief, he started out in politics with the Republican Party in California totally apathetic to his future. It was only after he defeated Jerry Voorhis that the machine tried to climb on his bandwagon by offering belated campaign contributions. They were not accepted. Until he ran for the Vice Presidency, he campaigned mainly on volunteer strength and money, yet managed to be one of the greatest vote-getters in his state's history.

There are those who profess to see a "change" between the Representative Nixon of 1946 and the Vice President Nixon of 1956. Any man of intelligence and perceptiveness develops and matures with time and experience. But in basic principles, and in the expression of those principles, Nixon has remained the same man. James Reston, writing for the New York *Times*, cited as an example of the "change" in Nixon his use of the quotation from Woodrow Wilson to which I refer in the final chapter. That quotation, significantly, can be found in speeches by Nixon going back several years. However, it is true that in specifics Nixon has tempered expression of his own opinions since January, 1953. As a man who respects the Constitution, Nixon has made his own views secondary to those of President Eisenhower. This is not change or compromise, but a reflection of the respect he holds for the President and for the office he holds.

A final word—and that of thanks to Rose Mary Woods, Dorothy Cox, and John Tretheway of the Vice President's staff for the time and effort they expended supplying me with material from the files. I need not, but will, add to this my thanks to Nora de Toledano who as always labored over the manuscript, organized material, and gave the best of editorial advice. The hardship was theirs; the blame or credit is mine.

CONTENTS

I. A MEASURE OF DECISION

For a man in politics, the choice between conscience and career is often a simple one. Conscience is the luxury of kings and newspaper columnists; a politician lives to be re-elected. Yet this was the choice which faced Representative Richard M. Nixon in the summer of 1948. There was a decision to be made, a road to be taken. If he chose the way of expediency, he would be destroying the fabric of his conscience; if he chose the way of conscience, he could be destroying a career which already promised much.

The Hiss Case had broken like a thunderclap over the nation. And in the formalistic way of American politics it had resolved itself into one echoing question: "Who is lying—Alger Hiss or Whittaker Chambers?" In time the issue became broader than the personal conflict of protagonist and antagonist, involving a whole concept of life. But in those hot August days only the innocent and the dedicated realized this. The evidence shows that from the start Richard Nixon understood the moral and political implications of the case. Without that understanding there would have been no problem.

Who was lying—Hiss or Chambers? Behind that easy question there lurked perils and complexities. People have forgotten the vast and powerful forces which from the start were lined up on the side of Hiss. Precise yet debonair, he was the very model of a model public servant. Park Avenue, Wall Street, and the Washington cocktail circuit echoed with his praises. Men of influence, stature, and probity—in government and the professions—took one horrified look at the first headlines and rushed to their desks to write or dictate letters of reassurance to Hiss.

Even to press the question, to seek a conclusive answer, was to confess an alliance with Satan. Members of the House Un-American Activities Committee, already bruised by years of criticism, had listened to Hiss and then hurried to shake his hand. Nixon alone had persisted in going ahead with the inquiry. The first week had produced only contradictory testimony which merely emphasized the dilemma.

"It would have been easy then," Nixon recalls, "to have dropped the case, patted Hiss on the back, and become a hero to his many friends and admirers. I recall that Mary Spargo, who had the unusual distinction of being friendly to the committee though a reporter for the Washington *Post*, came up to me after Hiss concluded his testimony and warned me that both the committee and I personally would be destroyed if we didn't get ourselves 'off the hook.' She said to me, 'Here's a chance to win some liberal support by repudiating Chambers and clearing Hiss. Virtually every one of the press corps is convinced that Hiss is telling the truth.' I told her we had an obligation to conduct further investigation in view of the very serious nature of the Chambers charges. 'Well, go ahead,' she said. 'But I warn you, you'd better be right or you're a dead duck.' "

Nixon reasoned that to back out would be taken as an admission that there was no case against Hiss, that he was innocent in the eyes of one of the most determined anti-Communists on the committee. Nixon's reputation for "fairness" would have skyrocketed, the quiet pressures would have been relaxed, and the growing campaign of vilification would suddenly have ended.

The price, perhaps, seemed small. And there was much at stake for Nixon. In less than two years as a congressman he had built up a national reputation. A year before, that grizzled veteran of the Washington wars, Speaker Joe Martin, had said, "Mr. Nixon is one of the ablest young men to come to Congress in many years." Other young congressmen whom he had organized into a potent operating unit looked to him for leadership. In the time that most men take to learn the ropes, he had left his mark on foreign, labor, and antisubversive legislation. His career and his effectiveness would be jeopardized if he persisted in the Hiss investigation and proved to be wrong.

Yet he had seen Hiss and Chambers on the witness stand. He had cross-examined both men. And with the sixth sense of a good trial lawyer, he had been convinced that, whatever the whole truth might be, Hiss was lying. If this were so, Nixon reasoned, then to drop the case would be a monstrous injustice to Chambers and a betrayal of his own trust as a member of Congress. He could drift with the tide, Nixon knew, but should he? Though his political opponents have zealously labored to question Nixon's moral nature, it is a strongly operative facet of his inner self. He could not put the problem lightly aside.

One day, while the headlines screamed and the columnists scolded, Richard Nixon climbed into his car and drove up to the small farm near York, Pennsylvania, where his parents had been living since his election to Congress. Among the old outbuildings was a reconverted washhouse, and Nixon sat there for hours, slumped on an ancient couch and staring into the empty fireplace. When his mother called him for meals, he called back, "Go ahead and eat—I'm not hungry." From time to time he wandered out for long, brooding walks. In a very literal sense he was wrestling with his soul.

"Why don't you drop the case, Richard?" his mother said to him. "No one else thinks Hiss is guilty."

"I've got a feeling Hiss is lying," he answered. "I've got to stick it out until I prove whether I'm right or not."

"Don't give in then," she said. "Do what you think is right."

The words were an echo of his childhood and of the days

when he had clerked in Frank Nixon's general store in the small California town of Whittier. Hannah Nixon had discovered that one of their customers was shoplifting. She had taken the problem to her husband, and Frank Nixon had said, "Call the police." She had discussed it with the leader of their Quaker meeting, and he had said, "Call the police." Hannah Nixon had refused; she could not bear to ruin a life. They had insisted that she was wrong. They had argued with her that it was her duty to inform the police. Looking for someone who would give her support, she had turned to Dick, her most serious and oldest surviving son. "Don't give in," he had said. "Do what you think is right." She had never informed the police—and now his words had come back to him.

At this point of crisis they were his measure of decision. He drove back to Washington determined to press for a conclusive answer to the question which plagued the nation—though the high and the mighty had no doubt of Hiss' innocence. In an office in New York a mimeograph machine was turning out copies of the letters which Hiss' friends had written to him. The letters, sent where they could do Hiss the most good, were a formidable display:

"If there is anything at all that I can do . . . I know that you will call on me," wrote Carl B. Spaeth, Dean of the Stanford law school and a former State Department colleague. Francis Sayre, U. S. representative on the UN Trusteeship Council felt "distressed and keenly regretful that you are being subjected to unfair and totally unjust accusations." Clarence Pickett, executive secretary of the American Friends Service Committee, suggested that Hiss' lack of "total recall" was a point in his favor. Former Secretary of War Robert P. Patterson reiterated his "trust and confidence." Senator Herbert H. Lehman expressed his "complete confidence in your loyalty" and found Hiss' testimony "forthright." Acting Secretary of State William Clayton also had "complete confidence" and offered his "heartiest congratulation." Ralph Bunche called the House hearings "an utterly shameless attempt to smear your good name." H. H. Fisher, chairman of the Hoover Library and Institute, deplored "this shocking and disreputable business." State Department officials, UN delegates, law professors, and business executives added to the chorus.

But the battle had been joined—it can almost be said by Nixon's act of will. In the days and weeks and months that followed, Hiss' guilt was proven beyond a peradventure of a doubt. The vital evidence was forced out of its hiding place. A jury submitted its verdict and a judge passed sentence on Alger Hiss. And Richard Nixon emerged from the furnace of the Hiss Case with his conscience unseared and his career intact. Even before the courts had sealed the fate of Hiss, the late Robert Sherwood, a strong New Dealer and the biographer of Franklin Delano Roosevelt and Harry Hopkins, had conceded that Nixon was "one of the most forward-looking members of our Congress."

From that point on, the wheels of history accelerated for Richard Nixon. He was marked by the Hiss Case and by the decision he had made. The Senate was the next logical station. And six years after he had taken the oath, a freshman in Congress, he was standing on the steps of the Capitol, a principal in the solemn ceremony which makes of two Americans a President and a Vice President. The rise was rapid, but it was not easy. The achievement was great, but the cost was greater.

His role in the Hiss Case had won for Nixon the unabashed hatred of the most indefatigable and subtle force in American politics. In the midst of the Presidential campaign, the enemy had struck—in a manner at once subtle and brash. Though he had triumphed, the smear still remained as he stood before the cheering crowds on the long day of the Inauguration. Among the cheers there were snickers—and they grew louder as Richard Nixon became the first Vice President to preside over the Cabinet, the first to sit as the President's deputy at meetings of the powerful National Security Council, the first Vice

President to demolish Throttlebottom and become a figure of stature and significance among those who make up the Executive.

In that time he has been under sharp scrutiny by both friend and foe. A whispering campaign of vast proportions has buzzed around him. Forged documents to impugn his honesty have been produced, exposed, and then quietly withdrawn. He has been simultaneously accused of being a supporter and a betrayer of Senator Joe McCarthy, a doctrinaire and an opportunist, an internationalist and an isolationist. (With his usual disregard for truth, Drew Pearson has stated blandly that Nixon voted *against* every foreign aid measure, when almost precisely the opposite is true.) It has been said that he is too subservient, or not subservient enough, to President Eisenhower. He has been depicted as a political wild man and as a crafty, conniving conspirator. When, for twenty-four hours after the President's heart attack, Nixon made himself unavailable to the press, Drew Pearson reported with a grandiose mendacity that he had spent the time plotting a seizure of power.

The debate has raged around Nixon—but few have bothered to know the man or to study the cold record. It is in the man and the record that Richard M. Nixon begins to assume dimension. No one can yet say if there is greatness in him, for greatness is a function of circumstances. But with or without circumstance Nixon represents an American phenomenon. It is as indigenous as an Indian fighter, as characteristic as a covered wagon, as unpretentious as apple pie. The elements of this phenomenon can be found in his heredity, his upbringing, his private and public life, his principles and his actions. But in life, as in art and politics, the whole is always greater than the sum of its parts. The valid story of Richard Nixon is an organic whole. It can only begin in the story of his family.

The American Success Story has standards as rigid as those of the soap opera. Under the code the hero must be a boy who rises from unmitigated poverty to great place. Or, being born to wealth and aristocracy, he must transcend such disadvantages to become a man of the people. Lincoln and Jefferson are the prototypes. Unfortunately, life seldom follows art—although the feature writers do. In a nation dominated by its middling classes, success picks its heroes at random, and triumph may come even to the son of an account executive.

Hannah Milhous Nixon expressed it much more directly. "A person has to stand on his own two feet in this world," she would say to her son. "What you make of yourself, and not your family, is what counts." Yet this statement of pragmatic truth, a motive force in the life of Richard Nixon, has its own built-in inaccuracies. What a man's family has been is always woven into the pattern of his personality. And though he may never mention it, the consciousness of his antecedents lives with him to plague or reassure in his moments of doubt. Every man is an image graven by himself and by his heredity.

From this point of view, and this point of view alone, the question of Richard Nixon's ancestry is significant and interesting. Of Scotch-Irish extraction, the predominant strain of early American colonization, his roots are deep in our history. Edward Nixon settled in America in the early Eighteenth Century. His two sons, John and George, fought in the

War for Independence. John was sheriff of Philadelphia and in that capacity gave the Declaration of Independence its first public reading. He rose to the rank of colonel in the Continental Army. George—private, ensign, and finally lieutenant—crossed the Delaware with Washington and took part in the Battle of Trenton. Eventually he settled in Ohio.

The records of the War Between the States show that George Nixon III, of Clinton County, enlisted with Company B, 73d Ohio Voluntary Infantry Regiment. He is buried at Gettysburg—one of the last to die in that terrible and decisive battle. His son, Samuel Brady Nixon, married Sally Ann Wadsworth, a descendant of the first American commando, General "Mad Anthony" Wayne. Their son, Francis Anthony Nixon, is Richard's father.

That the Nixons have fought their country's battles does not make them aristocrats. They were grass-roots Americans, farmers who worked the soil and drew their living from it. They were not wealthy; neither were they poor. In evaluating Richard Nixon there is another factor which, without diving like a loon for hidden compensations, may be of some importance. Frank Nixon was another type of characteristic American, the rolling stone. Tragedy—the death of his mother when he was seven—may have furnished the impetus. In any case, he quit school in the fourth grade to go to work as a farm hand, and from this followed his itinerancy.

"We farmhands usually had milk and bread for dinner," Frank Nixon recalls. "Fifty to seventy-five cents a day was just about tops in wages for a farmhand in those days." Restless by nature, extroverted, argumentative, and gregarious, he stayed put for a while and then set out to sample the world. The sampling was wide: glass worker, potter, painter ("I even painted Pullman cars at one time"), potato farmer, sheep rancher in Colorado, pioneer telephone linesman, motorman, roustabout in the oil fields, carpenter, and more in the course of his working lifetime.

At one time he was even a labor agitator. The Ohio winters

were bitter cold, the motorman stood in an open vestibule, and Frank Nixon literally froze his feet. Organizing the other motormen, he beat at the door of the state legislature demanding enclosed vestibules and better working conditions. This single sally into politics left its mark on him, and in the years that followed, his categorical political opinions echoed in the Nixon home.

By 1907 Frank Nixon had made his way to a southern California as yet unswathed in the frenetic glamor of the movie industry. He was a motorman again, but on the old red trolleys which linked Los Angeles and Whittier the job was a pleasant one. Living in Whittier, a Methodist among Friends, he was soothed by the placidity of the Quaker town, by its well-ordered streets and the gentle hubbub of its prosperity. The spirit of the men who had founded it in 1887 was still abroad in the town—the men who naming it Whittier after the New England Quaker poet may have had in mind his simple verse:

> We cross the prairies as of old
> The pilgrims crossed the sea,
> To make the West, as they the East,
> The homestead of the free.

For the first time the rolling stone came to rest. Then, on 15 February 1908—a date Frank Nixon recalls with nostalgia— he met Hannah Milhous. The Milhouses, like the Nixons rooted deep in the nation's pre-Revolutionary past, were Irish Quakers, a rare breed. A family Bible records that Thomas Milhous came from a Dublin meeting to Pennsylvania in the Seventeenth Century. Franklin Milhous had pulled up stakes in Indiana, leaving a home as four-square as their sturdy Quaker faith, and settled in Whittier ten years after its founding. He brought his wife Almira, his nine children, and his mother Elizabeth with him. (When she died at the age of ninety-six, the firm-willed matriarchal influence of Mrs. Milhous had spread over the town.) Four months and ten days after Frank and Hannah met, they were married and moved into the Milhous home. For a time, long enough to let their first son Harold be born, Frank Nixon worked as a foreman on the Milhous ranch. Then the wanderlust seized him again. The details of the Nixon family's travels are meager and perhaps irrelevant. They set up in the San Joaquin Valley briefly and then moved back to southern California, to Yorba Linda, where on the side of a barren hill Frank planted a lemon orchard. In later years there proved to be oil under the land, but the lemon grove was a failure from the start and eventually he gave it up to return to Whittier. In the decade of struggle before they returned, however, Richard Milhous Nixon was born, on 9 January 1913, to be followed two years later by Donald.

Those who analyze by remote control may draw some conclusions from the fact that throughout his elementary school days Dick Nixon was never tardy. It may be worthy of record that he was a bright child who cut his reading teeth on the daily newspapers and found them fascinating, that in three years at the Yorba Linda elementary school he covered four years' work, that he did his chores faithfully and without fuss. But another side to his character might tend to prove that there was in him certainly a little of the Tom Sawyer to balance the Cousin Sid.

The novelist Jessamyn West,* a cousin of the Nixons, reports that Dick liked to swim in Anaheim Ditch—dangerous for its steep sides and fast currents—in violation of the law and his mother's stern admonitions. What, Miss West wondered, would the Democrats make of the fact that "Richard and his older brother Harold defied the law and spent many a happy summer hour floating down the forbidden stream." The point of this observation is somewhat dimmed by Miss West's further recollection that his Sunday school teacher once remarked: "I expect that Richard Nixon will some day be

---

* Her book, *The Friendly Persuasion*, immortalizes her great-grandfather, who is also Richard Nixon's great-grandfather, a redheaded Irish Quaker who outraged his Meeting by buying an organ for his home.

President of the United States." Such prophecies have been made about boys who grew up to be butchers, bandits, and college presidents. They are usually said about Sunday school students who never drop buttons in the collection plate.

The Nixons returned to Whittier in the spring of 1922. Frank opened a country store and, since automobiles were becoming more of a commonplace, he installed a gasoline pump—one of the first in the area and perhaps his first stroke of sound business enterprise. The Nixons settled down, and though they continued to work hard, economic pressures began easing off. The store became a kind of neighborhood club, with Frank debating his customers on the political issues of the day and Mrs. Nixon soothing them.

Frank Nixon's argumentativeness was not destructive, however. Jessamyn West attests to the richly complex nature from which it stemmed and, indirectly, to its effect on young Richard. Her Cousin Frank, she recalls, taught Sunday school and "related his lessons to the life about us, to politics, local and national. His class was so popular it overflowed the space allotted to it and if I could have attended it a few more years I think I might have become a fair stateswoman myself." Dick Nixon never stood up in argument to his father, and he often counseled his brothers never to challenge Frank Nixon in debate. But he drew heavily in later years on the genuine and unreconstructed liberalism of his father's thinking.

Much has been made of the fact that Dick Nixon was a "serious boy"—as if this were somehow ominous. Though there is little evidence either way on this point, it is reasonable to suppose that he was. Both his youngest and his oldest brothers died during Richard's school years. The youngest, Arthur, whose death was sudden, had been very close to Dick in spite of their age difference. His older brother, Harold, was an invalid for several years before his death from tuberculosis, and many of his responsibilities fell to Dick. There was school, there were Quaker services at midweek and three times on Sunday, there was work at the store, there were violin and piano lessons. Years later Donald Nixon said, "None of us had too much time to play. Dick has had a lot to make him serious." Former classmates, prompted by his present position on the national scene, root in their memories for something to prove that even then his future was clear. The fact is, however, that Richard Nixon was brighter and more determined than most of his contemporaries, if no prodigy.

One episode points to the "Nixon method" that was to be— and to his lifelong love affair with facts. In the seventh grade he was chosen to take the affirmative in a debate whose subject was: *Resolved—That insects are more beneficial than harmful*. This maiden effort in public speaking frightened Dick Nixon, as it would have any child. But he sought out an etymologist uncle, stuffed himself with information, snowed under his opponents, and won the debate. It was the first of many debating victories. And it tells more about Nixon than his "seriousness," his high marks, or his perfect attendance record.

The high marks continued in high school and so did Dick Nixon's prowess as a debater. Though his two years at Fullerton High School were relatively uneventful, he won the Constitutional Oratorical Contest for the first time as a sophomore at Fullerton and was lauded in the 1928 yearbook for his "excellent work" as the sophomore representative of West Coast High Schools in the National Oratorical Contest. The subject, interestingly enough, was the U. S. Constitution, which had begun to fascinate him in the seventh grade and was the topic of many later speeches. The text of one of these speeches still exists, and for all its schoolboy rhetoric, it expresses a Constitutionalist faith which to this day is his. "It is our duty," he said in earnest peroration, "to protect this precious document, to obey its laws, to hold sacred its mighty principles, that our descendants may have that priceless heritage—our privileges under the Constitution."

In his junior year Dick Nixon transferred to Whittier High School. His mother had taken Harold to Prescott, Arizona, hoping the dry climate would cure his tuberculosis, and a larger share of the work in the store fell to Dick. He not only helped to keep the books but had full charge of the fruit and vegetable department—driving to the Los Angeles public market before sunrise to do the purchasing and then tending the store after school. His academic work, however, never suffered for this and he maintained the equivalent of an "A" average, and both in his junior and senior years won the Constitutional Oratorical Contest again. In an intelligence test for which the norm was 35, Nixon scored 59. O. C. Albertson, the principal at Whittier, recalls that "Dick was a marked man when he transferred to us. He was a leader in scholastic and student activities—a self-starter—very popular. I think of Dick as a 'fighting Quaker.' "

At graduation he received the California Interscholastic Federation Gold Seal Award for scholarship on his diploma and won the Harvard Award as "best all-around student," but turned down the opportunity to apply for a scholarship from Harvard University because he could not afford to go away to school at the time. He chose instead Whittier College, a quiet school of high academic standards, dedicated to Quaker ideals and George Fox's dream of a "Christian democracy." Dick Nixon was only seventeen when he began his freshman year, but the prodigious energy he showed in later years was already apparent. His capacity to learn, to assimilate, and to cut through to essentials was striking. Paul Smith, then a professor and now president of Whittier, still remembers Nixon's brief examination papers. "At first you thought that he couldn't answer the question in that short a space," he says. "But, by golly, he had gone to the heart of the problem and put it down simply."

Nixon graduated second in his class, but he also piled up an extracurricular record of unusual proportions. The tribute of Whittier's football coach for a man who won his freshman numeral and then sat on the Varsity bench for the rest of his college career is well known, but it bears repeating: "He was a second-string man. He played tackle and he played it well, but the kid was just too light. Weeks would go by and he wouldn't ever play a minute, but he'd hardly ever miss a practice, and he worked hard. He was wonderful for morale, because he'd sit there and cheer the rest of the guys, and tell them how well they'd played. To sit on the bench for four years isn't easy. I always figure, especially in the case of Dick who excelled in everything else, that kids like that have more guts than the first-string heroes."

That he excelled in other things is a simple matter of record. He was president of the freshman class. As the freshman star on the debating team, he helped defeat the University of Southern California, defending the proposition that *All Nations Should Adopt a Policy of Free Trade.* He won the *Reader's Digest* Southern Conference Extemporaneous Speaking Contest and in his senior year became the Southern California Intercollegiate Extemporaneous Speaking champion. He played leads in college plays. He was red-faced about a yearbook quip that he "left a trail blazed with fluttering feminine hearts." He traveled thousands of miles representing Whittier in debates as a member of the champion team of his college conference.

One episode has a certain amusing relevance to Nixon's later life. At the end of his sophomore year he ran for vice-president of the student body and won on a platform of "Impartial cooperation with the president." He became president, in his senior year, after a hard-fought campaign. In that office he embarked on a program of training for underclassmen, to prepare them for student leadership. The campus newspaper, of which he was a rather mediocre associate editor, found that during his term of office, "President Nixon" was "always progressive and with a liberal attitude," leading the school "through the year with flying colors."

Unlike the great secular universities, Whittier College had no fraternities, no sororities, no drinking clubs, not even a chapter of Phi Beta Kappa. But it did have the Franklins, a somewhat snobbish society wielding considerable power on the campus. With a group of other students, Nixon set out to break its monopoly on Whittier's social life by organizing the Orthogonians, a composite Greek word meaning "square-shooters." Its symbol was the square, the four corners standing for "Beans, Brawn, Brains, and Bowels." Nixon wrote its song, a kind of Three Musketeers tune entitled *Ecrassons l'Infame*, and became the Orthogonians' first president.

Dick Nixon did not graduate with honors. At the time Whittier considered such ostentation unseemly for a Quaker institution. But he stood second in his class and his extracurricular record was the sort which American institutions of learning value. He was, therefore, easily qualified for any graduate school. But he had his eye on the law. His mother says that this ambition was expressed when Nixon, then nine years old, read a newspaper account of the Teapot Dome scandal and remarked, "When I get big, I'll be a lawyer they can't bribe." If the story is apocryphal, it has its symbolic truth.

"The boy with the intellectual look above the eyebrows"— as the Whittier paper had referred to him—might have set his sights on Harvard or Yale. He chose, instead, Duke University's School of Law—attracted by the possibility of a tuition scholarship.

A warm letter of recommendation accompanied his bid for entrance and a scholarship to Duke Law School. His faculty adviser wrote: "At Whittier, Richard Nixon displayed a rich sense of humor, human understanding, personal eloquence, and a marked ability to lead. He is intellectually honest, modest, and youthfully enthusiastic. If he has any handicap, it is his lack of sophistication." President Walter F. Dexter of Whittier introduced Nixon to Dean H. Claude Horack in even warmer terms. "I believe that [Nixon] will become one of America's important, if not great, leaders," he wrote.

In September, 1934, Richard Nixon, a young man of twenty-one, thin, serious-faced, the jowls which so delight the political cartoonists not yet upon him, determined, and hopeful, looked at the lovely and luxurious campus which tobacco millions had created. Years later a classmate named Hoover Taft, Jr. (no kin, no Republican), said, "Dick was there for only one purpose, and that was to train himself to be the best lawyer in the country."

The law as she is taught in America, however, is more an ordeal by grind than an indoctrination in jurisprudence. For Dick Nixon the difficulties were multiplied. To hold his tuition scholarship he was required to maintain an average of B or better. His family could send him only thirty-five dollars a month toward rent, food, clothing, books, and incidental expenses. Even at depression prices he could not afford the relative luxury of a dormitory room, and the thirty-five cents an hour he made doing research for Dean Horack—a job and a salary he truly appreciated—made his lot only slightly less penurious.

He solved the rent problem by sharing a room in an old farmhouse with three other equally economical law students —William R. Perdue who is now vice-president of the Ethyl Corporation; Fred S. Albrink, who made his career in the Navy, holds the rank of captain, and is chairman of the Board of Review in the Judge Advocate General's office; and Lyman Brownfield, who has a prosperous law practice in Columbus, Ohio. The ramshackle farmhouse was a mile through the woods to the Duke campus, a mile that was muddy or dusty as the weather dictated, and the four students paid about fifty dollars a year for the back room.

It was, as Brownfield describes it, a "pretty crude place with no running water and no heat other than an old laundry stove." They called it Whippoorwill Manor, to make up for some of its drawbacks. "It was cold on some of those winter nights," Brownfield says. "Those old laundry stoves were made of thin metal that would heat up fast and cool off just as quickly. At bedtime we'd stuff the thing with papers and get it going while we undressed and hopped into bed. But it had its pleasant side too. A good part of the year was mild and those woods are lovely in the fall and spring."

They worked hard—Perdue, Brownfield, and Nixon were graduated the top men of the class, in that order—and there was little time for recreation. Now and then Nixon would take time out to listen to the music of Johnny Long and Les Brown, two undergraduates who led orchestras which have since made the big time. "Old Nixon used to like to hear them play," says Captain Albrink, "but he'd only hang around fifteen minutes or so and then he'd hit the books again." There was handball, the occasional luxury of a football game, and a few dates. "Dick wasn't allergic to girls," Brownfield recalls. "He liked them—as all of us did. But we just didn't have the money, and the dates were few and far between."

In his second year at Duke Law, Dick Nixon did what by then came naturally. He ran for the presidency of the Duke Bar Association, an organization of the school's students and the most sought-after office. He won. He was on the Law Review staff, and between his second and third years remained at Duke to write a full-length article for *Law and Contemporary Problems* as one of two members of the entire Law School student body chosen to write articles that year. As a senior, he was elected to the Order of the Coif, a national honorary society to which only the top 10 per cent of the country's law students are qualified for membership. Most important for Nixon, however, was the warm friendship which resulted from his research work for Dean Horack. Nixon specialized in taxation, but his main interest at Duke was Constitutional law—his classmates considered him a "conservative liberal"— and the respect for the Constitution which he had demonstrated in his high school days was nourished and matured in long conversations with his teacher.

In 1937 Richard Nixon got his law degree from Duke and prepared to face the great world. His next contact with Duke came many years later—and it was an acid one. In the spring of 1954 the trustees informed Nixon that they were awarding him the honorary degree of doctor of laws, and he was invited to deliver the Commencement address. Nixon's attachment to Duke was genuine and deep, and he accepted the invitation readily, having turned down about thirty other such invitations. Faculty approval of the award was expected *pro forma*—in the school's fifty-year history it had never overruled the trustees' choice for the annual Commencement honors. But the Duke faculty voted to refuse Nixon the honorary degree.

What had happened was simple enough. Barely one sixth of the 622 faculty members attended what was to have been a routine meeting. But that one sixth consisted largely of those faculty members who bore Nixon a political grudge for exposing Alger Hiss and the Communist infiltration of the Roosevelt-Truman administrations. They kept their opposition to Nixon a secret, acting as a caucus, until the meeting—and then they were able to outvote the rest of their colleagues present. None of the law school voted with the anti-Nixon group.

This victory for academic freedom raised a storm among the alumni and contributions to Duke fell off. Said one prominent alumnus after the news of the vindictive slap at Duke's most illustrious alumnus had leaked out: "That Hiss thing stuck in their craw. They don't like to have that proved on one of the boys." And Horack, now Dean Emeritus of the law school, added, "I thought educators would be above that."

That they weren't came as no surprise to Richard Nixon. His comparatively short education in politics had been more than liberal.

3. THE GREAT WORLD

In the spring of 1937 Richard Nixon tucked his diploma under his arm and took a look at the world. What he saw was hardly reassuring. The Roosevelt Administration was in the period of the Great Hiatus between relief and rearmament, euphemistically called the Recession. Convinced that he had cured the nation's economic illness, Franklin D. Roosevelt began to shut off the outpouring of vast funds to the WPAs and the PWAs. But his own Bureau of Labor Statistics was reporting that well over 11,000,000 Americans were out of work—a fact which few remember today. Industrial production was slumping almost as fast as the stock market, and in a two-month period over 850,000 workers lost their jobs. The country may have feared nothing but fear—but according to the great liberal historian Charles A. Beard, the "economic collapse was startling to President Roosevelt and his advisers."

To a young man ready to embark on his career, the prospect ahead seemed one of perpetual economic crisis. Only a prophet could have foreseen Mr. Roosevelt's brilliant shift from isolationism to interventionism—a policy about-face which set the wheels of heavy industry rolling again. For young lawyers, however, there was one solution—government service, which seemed to have an unlimited capacity for absorbing junior legal talent. This solution Dick Nixon discussed with his friend and adviser, Dean Horack, who volunteered his good offices to get him a position with the Justice Department.

But Horack also had some advice to offer. He and Nixon had frequently discussed the subject of politics as a career, and Nixon had given that possibility more than casual thought. Horack told him, "Dick, if you're really interested in politics, go back to your home town and establish yourself in a law firm." At first Dick Nixon had demurred. Service with the FBI appealed to him, and Horack had even written a letter of recommendation to Director J. Edgar Hoover, calling to his attention "one of the finest young men, both in character and ability, that I have ever had the opportunity of having in my classes." Nixon took and passed the FBI examination, but he decided eventually not to join up if he was accepted. Hoover nevertheless likes to consider Nixon "one of my boys," a designation, Nixon says, "which I am very proud to bear."

Dr. Horack's advice, and his own predilections for the steppingstone of private law practice, prevailed. There was, however, one catch. He had not made application to take the California Bar Examination, scheduled for that summer. Again Dean Horack came to his aid. In a letter to Professor James E. Brenner he asked for advice. Could anything be done which would permit "one of our very best students" to take the examination without waiting for any subsequent one. Through Brenner's intervention, Dick Nixon's name was added to the list of candidates, and he returned to Whittier to prepare.

It is characteristic of Nixon that, faced with obstacles, he feels like a pessimist and acts like an optimist. On 3 July 1937, he wrote to a friend at Duke that the "Bar Exam Cram Course" in Los Angeles had started in March so that he would have to double-cram by crowding five months' work into two. "I seriously doubt that I can get up the stuff in good enough shape in two months but I'm going to try," he said. "Tell Dean Horack, therefore, that the first Duke graduate to take the California Bar Exam has a darn good chance to fail it the first time." And Horack answered, "Don't worry . . . they will have to flunk all of them if they don't let you by." Nixon's fears were not realized, though a bout of influenza almost put him out of the running. He was one of the 46 per cent who passed the examination, and he was sworn in as a member of the bar before the State Supreme Court in San Francisco on 9 November 1937.

Nixon returned to Whittier after the ceremony and joined the law firm of Wingert & Bewley. He had sought the job, but in a sense the job had sought him too. The firm had been looking for a young lawyer to handle the trial work, to fill in as an expert on Constitutional law, and to take over the trying job of preparing briefs. Bewley, who doubled as city attorney, also wanted a man who could serve as his assistant and deputy in that job, and who could get along with the ever-touchy City Council. There is no record of any weighty Constitutional punditing by Nixon, but in all the other departments he fully satisfied the firm of Wingert & Bewley. In a year they had made him a partner, and the firm's name was changed to Wingert, Bewley & Nixon—which it remained until Dick Nixon was elected to Congress in 1946 and took the almost unprecedented step among lawyer-congressmen of resigning his partnership.

As a trial lawyer Richard Nixon was neither flashy nor dramatic, and he never badgered witnesses; but in cross-examination, Tom Bewley says, "he always seemed to be way ahead of the witness and to anticipate what answers the witness would make." His strong point with juries was his ability to marshal his arguments cogently and to speak directly to them. As a writer of briefs he startled Bewley. "Give him a problem at noon," Bewley has said, "he would pull down the books and dictate the brief. He would have approved the final draft, meticulous as he was, before I could have looked up the books." But there was one side of law work which he actively disliked. Quaker-born and Quaker-bred, living a life under the twin disciplines of work and duty, he had never seen at arm's reach the seamy side of human relations. He could be tolerant or stern, but he never handled a divorce case without acute embarrassment over the details of conjugal behavior which it was his job to probe.

During those early law years, Bewley says, Nixon put in a sixteen-hour day for days on end, working late at night and pacing up and down his office, his shoulders hunched up, as he thought through a legal problem. But there were some beer and skittles to his life. He was active in civic organizations, becoming president of the Whittier 20-30 Club, a kind of Junior Chamber of Commerce, and a trustee of Whittier College. He often took time out in the evening to participate in the amateur productions of Whittier's "little theater" group. It was at rehearsals for the George S. Kaufman and Alexander Woollcott play, *The Dark Tower*, that he met Thelma Patricia Ryan, a tall, redheaded, gentle girl, quiet and friendly and unassuming.

Pat Ryan's life story was, like Dick Nixon's, torn from the pages of the workaday American saga. She was Irish on her father's side, Connecticut Irish. Her mother was of German stock. Like many Californians, she had been born out of the state—in Nevada—and had been brought to the Coast when she was a baby. Her father bought a small farm near Artesia, a little town some eighteen miles from Los Angeles, and the Ryans settled down to what must have seemed like a quiet life. It didn't work out that way.

"Both of my parents died before I had grown up," she has written, "and when I finished high school I went to work in a bank at Artesia to earn enough money to complete my education. But in 1930 I learned that some elderly friends of my relatives in Connecticut were driving home from California, and I offered to be their chauffeur. That's how I got East and, luckily, got a job in the laboratory of a hospital near New York City. I did office work and then X-ray work in the laboratory for two years before returning home to attend the University of Southern California. I had a research fellowship, I graded papers, and I worked week ends and holidays in a department store until I was graduated. I had studied merchandising, but after graduation I went to Whittier to teach school. I don't know just why, but I usually tell people that the reason I went to Whittier was to meet Dick."

When she met Richard Nixon, she was teaching commercial subjects—typing and shorthand—at Whittier and nourishing a vague desire to become an actress. (As a student at USC, she had even played microscopic bit parts in two movies, *Becky Sharp* and *Small Town Girl*.) Their decision to get married was not long in coming, but it was not until 21 June 1940, well over two years later, that they had saved up enough money to "pool our savings to buy a wedding ring and go on our honeymoon." Dick Nixon continued to practice law and Pat to teach.

The first year of marriage was happy and uneventful. There was a Presidential election, and Nixon campaigned for Wendell Willkie, the Republican candidate, but the passions of that campaign did not cut deep into the pattern of his daily living. There was a war in Europe, and Great Britain was fighting for her life against the Luftwaffe, but in the Quaker town of Whittier it must have seemed a little remote. President Roosevelt had promised "again and again and again," in a speech of ringing sincerity, that American boys would not be sent overseas.

Pearl Harbor interrupted a peaceful Sunday and changed the lives of millions of Americans. The war struck home. Dick Nixon was caught up in the sudden upsurge of national feeling. As a Quaker, he could have claimed exemption from military service, but he felt the need to participate in the national effort by joining the beehive of bureaucratic activity on the Potomac. Nixon went to Washington and found his niche in the OPA section of the Office of Emergency Management. Ironically, the man who hired him was Thomas I. Emerson, a member of the International Juridical Association with Alger Hiss, a member (and subsequently president) of the National Lawyers Guild which has been characterized as the "legal bulwark of the Communist Party," a chronic joiner of Communist fronts, and today a professor of law at Yale.

The meeting between Emerson and Nixon, however, was brief and routine. (Years later Emerson was to testify before the House Un-American Activities Committee as a voluntary witness against the Mundt-Nixon bill.) There was a crying need for lawyers to establish some order in the rationing regulations; Nixon's manner and background were more than adequate for requirements. "I hired him on the spot," Emerson says today. "He had an excellent record." To take the job in OPA Nixon gave up a law practice which by then was paying him over 6000 dollars a year, for a desk job at a salary of 3200 dollars—a substantial slash for a newly married young man who had no backlog of wealth. But working on OPA routine did not satisfy Nixon's sense of obligation to take part in the war effort.

He has since then summed up his feelings about OPA—and made them public in a manner which belies the assertion by the dirty-nail press and its respectable counterparts that he has kept his OPA employment "secret." "In OPA I learned respect for the thousands of hard-working government employees and an equal contempt for most of the political appointees at the top. I saw government overlapping and government empire-building first hand." J. Paul Marshall, his closest friend in the OPA office, the only other Republican, and incidentally a descendant of the great Chief Justice, attests to the fact that this is no hindsight on Nixon's part. "He just felt that we needed sounder thinking than we had in government in those days," he says. "We used to talk about that."

In a matter of months Nixon had decided that he was wasting his time in OPA. He was young and vigorous, in excellent health, and consumed by the feeling that he was not doing enough. Waiving his military exemption, he applied for a commission in the Navy and, on 2 September 1942, he was assigned to active duty as a lieutenant j.g. After training at Quonset,

Rhode Island, he made the mistake of applying for sea duty —and was sent forthwith to an unfinished base at Ottumwa, Iowa. Pat joined him there, getting a job as a bank teller until in May 1943 after again applying for sea duty he was assigned to the South Pacific Combat Air Transport Command (SCAT), serving at Guadalcanal, Bougainville, and Green Island. He was an operations officer, not a combat sailor—but at Bougainville he was under bombardment twenty-eight nights out of thirty. (Of this, he later wrote to his mother: "The only thing that really bothered me was lack of sleep and the centipedes"—sentiments shared by many others who took part in the dismal Pacific campaigns.)

A fellow Navy officer describes Nixon in those days: "If you saw Henry Fonda in *Mister Roberts* you know how Lieutenant Dick Nixon looked the first time I met him on a coral atoll off Bougainville in 1943," says Edward J. McCaffrey, now a Democratic postmaster at Concord, Massachusetts. "Nick was a Navy orphan, officer-in-charge of a unit without precedent, but with a mission."

McCaffrey continues: "Nick, a full lieutenant, and a j.g. named Jim Stewart, with a dozen enlisted men, radio operators, and flight operations rates, would be given transportation to an island completely unequipped except for a few hand tools. Left to their own resources, they were expected to establish a makeshift base for the DC-3s in a matter of days. And they did just that. How they did it, I'll never know, though I saw them operate on several different islands over a period of months. To set up their operation, Nick's outfit needed matériel and the most basic building supplies were precious. Some of the stuff they procured was 'liberated,' but most of it Nick wangled out of units better equipped than his. A single sheet of plywood would set in motion for him a chain reaction of swaps that in a couple of days would have his unit housed and operating.

"Nick was a worker. He was tireless. But when he spoke he made an awful lot of sense. He had no more rank than most

of us, he was our age generally speaking, but he commanded
a lot of respect from the guys with whom he came in contact.
When things got a bit hectic, he never lost his head. No matter how badly things got fouled up Nick got his part of the
operation straightened out and he did it without a lot of
hullaballoo."

His job in the South Pacific did not merely consist of setting up operations bases for the DC-3s. Planes had to be loaded
and unloaded—and in a rush. On 24 January 1944, for example, he received a message from Guadalcanal that thirty
planes carrying 135,000 pounds of a new type of rocket bomb
would arrive at his Bougainville base. In six hours he and his
nine men were to unload these planes, and "bomb up" combat
planes which were taking part in the great strike against Ra-
baul. The planes were then to be sent back to Guadalcanal
loaded with the litter cases who were casualties of a Japanese
raid on Bougainville the night before. This, in the Navy, is
enlisted men's work, but Lieutenant Nixon stripped off his
shirt and pitched in on the grueling physical labor. The job
was done.

He is also credited with setting up the only hamburger
stand in the South Pacific—a little snack stand known throughout the area as "Nixon's Snack Shack," located right near the
air strip on Green Island, where tired fliers could get coffee,
sandwiches, and fruit juice free. Somehow Nixon was able
to get the food from a Navy supply depot on the other end of
the island, "by trading everything from captured Japanese
rifles to introductions to the Army nurses who arrived to take
care of the casualties." On the side, he also set up an informal
school for the enlisted men—a typical mixture of farm boys,
slum kids, and wealthy boys from New York, California,
Nebraska, New Mexico, or Indiana—where he gave them a
course of instruction in business law.

One legend emerges from the Nixon tour of duty. On the
transport to New Caledonia, and at the various air stations to
which he was assigned, he had a reputation for never losing

his temper and never losing at poker. "There are a hundred Navy officers who will tell you that Nick never lost a cent at poker," says one of his fellow officers. "Nixon shared whatever he had," he adds irrelevantly, "food, liquor, and money. And I never saw an enlisted man who didn't like him."

Dick Nixon's fifteen months in the South Pacific ended when he was transferred to Fleet Air Wing 8 at Alameda, California, and from there was assigned on special orders to the Navy Bureau of Aeronautics. As the war came to an end, his legal training was once more put to use. The Navy assigned him to winding up active contracts with such aircraft firms as Bell and Glenn Martin, which earned him a letter of commendation for saving the government millions of dollars.

Then, in November 1945, Lieutenant Commander Richard Nixon waited impatiently in Baltimore to get his discharge. Like the preponderance of men in his position, he wanted to get out of the service. But there was also the great question: What now? His job with the OPA was open to him—he had left Washington on a military furlough. He could go back to his law firm in Whittier. Or he could strike out anew. While he pondered the alternatives, events and circumstances were deciding the question for him. A telegram was the instrument of fate.

4. THE MYTHOLOGY OF '46

History, Maxwell Anderson points out in several of his more memorable plays, is written by the victor. This was so in the days of Elizabeth the Queen and Franklin Delano Roosevelt. But the mythologists of certain newspapers have reversed the pattern. Feeding on each other's fabrications, they convert every defeat into fodder for new whispering campaigns against the victor. The telegram which changed the course of Richard Nixon's life, on that November day in 1945, was the first step down the road to an unprecedented political career. But the typewriter pundits, with calculated hindsight, have so garbled the facts, and given them such an overlay of fiction, that only painstaking research can set them in order.

In the fall of 1946 Richard M. Nixon, a political unknown, defeated Horace Jeremiah Voorhis, who had held his seat in the United States House of Representatives for five terms, by a plurality of 15,592 votes. The only mention of the campaign in the New York *Times* was on Election Day plus One, when the final figures were published. Coverage, in point of fact, seemed like wasted effort, despite the great Voorhis reputation, for he had done so well in the primaries that the experts conceded him the election from the very start. The Wednesday-morning quarterbacks were satisfied to chalk up the defeat as one more casualty of that year's great Republican sweep. And Jerry Voorhis himself, no man to mince words if he felt aggrieved, flatly stated that "overconfidence" was the cause of his downfall.

The myth of the 1946 campaign began to develop only after Nixon had given impetus to the Hiss investigation and taken strong exception to President Truman's reiterated "red herring" red herring. The young congressman from California had become a national figure—and those who sneered that he saw a Communist under every bed now looked for a devil under Nixon's. The strategy is as old as politics, and no party has a monopoly of it. In Nixon's case the outraged opposition could find nothing sordid in his personal life. Undaunted, they invented a horrendous account of the 1946 campaign and propagated it so feverishly that it has become an article of faith among anti-Nixonites.*

This is the story of the 1946 campaign as it really happened, not as it "must have" happened. The facts are important as a case study in the Nixon method—and in the method against Nixon.

In August 1945, twenty-six newspapers in California's Twelfth Congressional District carried what amounted to an advertisement on page one. It had come in the mail as a publicity handout, and the papers had printed it as a curiosity:

> WANTED: Congressman candidate with no previous political experience to defeat a man who has represented the district in House for ten years. Any young man, resident of district, preferably a veteran, fair education, no political strings or obligations and possessed of a few ideas for better-

* A most assiduous propagator of the 1946 myth has been Ernest Brashear, a West Coast labor reporter. Early in the 1952 Presidential campaign, Brashear gave the fabrication its most extended treatment in *The New Republic:* "Almost immediately Nixon took off on the issue of Communism and managed to give the impression that Voorhis, the liberal, was indistinguishable from a Communist Party member because he had received unsolicited endorsements from a few organizations in which Communists were active . . . More important were the anonymous telephone calls that citizens throughout the Twelfth District began to receive. 'This is a friend of yours, but I can't tell you my name,' the unknown voice would say. 'I just wanted you to know that Jerry Voorhis is a Communist'. . . It worked." Sundry hatchetmen of the New York *Post* have made the charge even stronger since then.

ment of country at large, may apply for the job. Applicants will be reviewed by 100 interested citizens who will guarantee support but will not obligate the candidate in any way.

The one hundred interested citizens were no money-bags cabal, as some would have it, but Republicans who had grown weary of seeing all comers defeated by the wealthy and personable Jerry Voorhis. This group, as *The Saturday Evening Post* later reported, was "a political and economic cross-section of the area which sprawls from the southern border of Los Angeles to the foothills of the San Gabriel Mountains," and "it represented small businessmen, farmers, professional men, commuters, citrus ranchers, laborers, housewives, and career women."

The "advertisement," however, had no tangible results. There were candidates in plenty—but not the type of candidate the Committee of One Hundred was seeking. In short order committee members turned down an ex-Democrat-ex-Socialist who offered to turn Republican, a smog expert, a politician who talked of keeping the "Jews and the niggers" out of the district, and the usual collection of hopeless young hopefuls. It was then that the late Herman L. Perry (a banker, *maxima culpa sua*) thought of Dick Nixon, whom he knew, and sent off a telegram to Baltimore asking Nixon to call long distance. Over the telephone he put two questions to Nixon: "Are you a Republican and are you available?"

"I guess I'm a Republican," Nixon is reported to have said. "I voted for Dewey in 1944." * There is no doubt that he declared himself available.

"Fly out here right away," Perry told Nixon.

---

* Anti-Nixon writers have spun a fanciful web about this purported answer. Richard Rovere, Washington correspondent for *The New Yorker*, took to the pages of *Harper's* to argue that Nixon had not been a Republican, has no political principles, and was merely being opportunistic. Others have argued the same point and like Rovere have never bothered to make a routine check. The facts: Nixon registered as a Republican on 5 June 1938, campaigned for Willkie in 1940, and remained a registered Republican until he lost his franchise by moving to Washington in 1942.

Seventy-seven members of the committee were assembled when Dick Nixon arrived. In ten minutes he stated his case. He stood for "a return to individual freedoms and all that private initiative can produce," he said, and he promised "an aggressive campaign on the platform of progressive liberalism [the word "progressive" had not yet been tainted by Gideon's Army] designed to return our district to the Republican Party." As he spoke, the committee looked him over. They saw a young, pleasant-faced man whose slightly mumpy cheeks and thrust-out nose took the curse off his handsomeness. They liked his directness of speech, and they were impressed by that indescribable quality which promises success in politics. They voted for Nixon, 55 to 22—and on the second ballot made it unanimous.

Thinking about it years later, Dick Nixon remarked, "Voorhis looked impossible to defeat. He was intelligent, experienced, he had a national reputation and came from a well-known California family. Why did I take it? I'm a pessimist, but if I figure I've got a chance, I'll fight for it. And I thought this was as good a time as any to get into politics."

Before he made his final decision, he talked it over with Pat. Their financial future, after all, was something to be seriously considered. Pat Nixon had worked at various jobs throughout the war, saving what she could. To this they had added Dick's allotments and what he had been able to put aside from his service pay. They had earmarked this sum of 10,000 dollars for a payment on a home—and for his new start in civilian life. "We'll gamble half of it on the election," they decided. And gamble it they did; the Nixon 1946 campaign was run on a shoestring, leaning heavily on volunteer help, for the scads of "big money" from "big business" materialized only in the anti-Nixon myths of later years. Indeed, Pat Nixon recalls the time she wept because they had no campaign funds for stamps to mail their campaign literature. Even the Republican County Finance Committee maintained a hands-off attitude on the grounds that financial assistance to Nixon would be a waste of money since he couldn't possibly win. After the campaign, however, there were numerous offers of funds "to help meet any deficit" in the campaign kitty, offers which Nixon was happy to turn down.

On 19 March 1946, Richard Nixon filed in both the Democratic and Republican primaries—as did Jerry Voorhis. This, in California, was and is standard operating procedure. Under the state's system of cross-filing, candidates try to knock out their opponents by capturing both nominations. The Nixons rented a small office in a dusty old building in Whittier's downtown section. They borrowed desks, chairs, tables, office equipment—and Hannah Nixon gave them an old leather sofa which Dick's brother Don hauled to the office in his grocery truck. Pat Nixon and her high school friend, Marion Budlong, ran the office and handed out the campaign literature which Nixon had printed up at his own expense. They were elated at the demand for this literature until they learned that the opposition had pulled one of the oldest tricks in politics, sending in "volunteers" who asked for bunches of pamphlets and then destroyed them. Until he could buy civilian clothes, Dick Nixon campaigned in his uniform. The first suit, a grey one, fitted badly. He bought a second suit, this time of the conventional blue, and sold the grey one—putting the money into the campaign kitty.

Right up through the primaries it seemed like a losing battle. Voorhis walked off with the Democratic nomination and won enough votes in the Republican primary to give him a 7000-vote over-all lead. "The election is in the bag for Voorhis," said the professionals—and the Committee of One Hundred shrugged its collective shoulders, convinced that they had picked a loser. But Nixon tucked his pessimism in his pocket and set out on a door-to-door campaign of the Twelfth District's 200,000 voters. His first real break came, oddly enough, because Voorhis was a methodical politician. In February 1946, Pat Nixon had given birth to their first child,

'Tricia. It was Voorhis' custom to send a government pamphlet, *Baby Care*, to all new parents in his district.

The one he sent to the Nixons, however, had a note attached. "Congratulations," it read. "I look forward to meeting you soon in public." Dick Nixon politely thanked Voorhis—and then challenged him to a series of debates on the issues of the campaign. The professional politicians shrieked in anguish. Didn't Nixon know that Voorhis had won his first election by challenging his opponent to debate and then taking him? "I'll risk it," said Nixon. "If I don't carry the fight to Voorhis, this campaign will never get off the ground." Nixon, of course, was right. For Voorhis, as he admits himself, had lost touch with his district—a failing common to all legislators who get so immersed in the national picture that they forget the viewpoint of their constituents. In Washington, Voorhis was a big name—but in California the voters hardly knew what he stood for. Nixon prepared for his debates with Voorhis as he had prepared his college debates—by immersing himself in the record, in every speech Voorhis had delivered, and in a book on money which he quoted back at Voorhis with devastating effect. Good or bad, it was a record of which few of the constituents were aware.

Jerry Voorhis was—and may still be—an earnest, pleasant, if somewhat humorless man, given to great soul-searchings and admissions of error (today he would be classified as an "egghead"), a doctrinaire thinker more interested in issues than in people. He considered himself a "Christian socialist," and he had in fact been a registered member of the Socialist Party before the New Deal captured its program. He had entered politics as an EPIC man, under the tutelage of Upton Sinclair, and had never shaken loose from some of the "funny money" principles of that frenetic movement. He was elected in 1936, when Franklin D. Roosevelt carried everything before him except those two states—and had taken the brunt of Communist attack by serving on the House Un-American Activities Committee and sponsoring the Foreign Agents Registration

Act—and then won left-wing plaudits by resigning from the committee with a blast at Red-hunters.

His constituents did not know that he had fought to socialize the Federal Reserve System or advocated nationalization of the oil industry. He was closely associated with the National Citizens- and the CIO-Political Action Committees on the national level. In a year when the Republican slogan was "Had enough?" he called for even more, angering the housewives who were fed up with meat rationing and OPA controls. The voters could not understand why he had failed to vote against a bill cutting veterans' compensation—or why he had introduced a bill of his own which sought to make veterans' disability payments loans instead of outright grants. To top it all, he favored restrictions on grain for use in the manufacture of liquor. For comic relief, there was the bill bearing his name—one of the few Voorhis succeeded in getting through Congress—which transferred control of the rabbit industry from the Interior to the Agriculture Department.

It was this record which Nixon used in his speeches and in his debates with Voorhis. "Had enough?" Nixon repeated and then stressed the socialist aspects of the Voorhis program and its general left-wing character. (If this be naughty, then Nixon pleads guilty.) The "whispering campaign" that Voorhis was a Communist is a fairly recent invention of the typewriter pundits. As late as 1947 Voorhis had complained only that the whispers against him were that he hadn't "done anything for the district"—and he admitted that it was "at least partly true." Of communism the mentions were so few and so fleeting as to be negligible. The fact is, as Nixon points out, that "communism was not the issue at any time in the '46 campaign. Few people knew about communism then, and even fewer cared." As Nixon had predicted, it was the five debates which catapulted Nixon forward in that first fight for a seat in Congress.

The candidates spoke before packed houses—Voorhis, as he says himself, "dull" and weighed down by the sense that the public would never be able to understand what he was talking about, and Nixon persuasive, carrying the attack to his opponent and showing the ease which years on the debate platform had given him. The first debate sparked the Nixon campaign —and Voorhis left the platform feeling bewildered, discouraged, and tired. He was just fresh from Washington, and Nixon had already put in weeks of grueling campaigning, but the difference between the two men was remarked by the voters.

The format of the debates was always the same. Each of the speakers addressed the audience for fifteen minutes and then went into open discussion. Nixon, *The Saturday Evening Post* has reported, "kicked off by asking Voorhis if he was endorsed by the PAC. Voorhis denied this categorically. In long strides the challenger crossed the stage and thrust a paper bearing the list of candidates endorsed by the National Citizens Political Action Committee under Voorhis' nose, commanding him to read it aloud. After an understandable pause, he replied that he didn't know Nixon meant *that* PAC list. Voorhis said he meant that the CIO-PAC had not endorsed him, but Nixon then pointed out—by reading off the names of officers of CIO-PAC and NC-PAC—that in many cases the leaders of the two organizations were the same. Not only was Voorhis doing some fancy hair-splitting, Nixon observed, but also this was the first time Voorhis had mentioned in his denials the CIO-PAC, which indeed had not endorsed him, as opposed to the NC-PAC, which had."

For the last Nixon-Voorhis debate, at San Gabriel Mission, the crowds overflowed the hall and amplifiers were needed to carry the speakers' voices to several hundred people who stood outside. Contributions had begun to flow in, often in the form of a crumpled bill or two pressed into the hand of a volunteer after a speech. Very few contributions were as high as 100 dollars. The professionals were elbowed aside and the amateur politicians handled everything, dreaming up slogans ("Put the Pin in PAC"), writing newspaper handouts, mailing out litera-

ture, canvassing from door to door. A district which had
been apathetic came to life. Nixon's victory was overwhelming—Voorhis did not even carry his home town—and he had
proved one of his favorite maxims: The greater the risk, the
greater the opportunity.

All that remained of the campaign—the terrible, terrible
campaign, according to those who know nothing about it but
what they read in today's papers—were the closing statements
of victor and vanquished. ". . . I have given the best years
of my life to serving this district in Congress," said Voorhis.
"By the will of the people that work is ended. I have no re-
grets about the record I have written . . ." In a manner as
standard and ritualistic Nixon answered: ". . . I do not consider this a personal triumph. Instead, the vote of the people
. . . was a clear mandate for a program of action by the new
Congress . . ."

There is one interesting postscript to the 1946 election.
Voorhis returned to Washington to wind up his affairs. On 7
December 1946, he wrote Richard Nixon a long and generous
letter:

> . . . I remember most poignantly the time in late December
> of 1936 when I first came to Washington as a new Congress-
> man. Little did I realize then all that the job entailed, the long
> hours of very hard and frequently thankless work, the many
> periods of frustration when one was unable to get the things
> done which he believed most necessary for the country, as
> well as those times of encouragement when something worth-
> while seemed to have been accomplished.
>
> During the ten years of my service I came to have a pro-
> found respect for the Congress of the United States and to
> realize the critical importance of its work, not only for the
> future of our country, but for the future of the whole world
> . . . It becomes more and more evident that the one essential
> bulwark of the people's liberties in such a nation is the vigor
> and effectiveness of the national legislature.
>
> If that national legislature occupies its proper place as a
> coequal branch of government, and especially if it puts forth

and enacts into law a program calculated to meet the nation's present and future problems, the future of freedom will be safe . . .

The long and short of this letter is simply to say, as I said in my newspaper release after the election at home, that I sincerely wish you well as you undertake the tremendous responsibilities which will soon be yours.

. . . I want you to know that I will be glad to be of any help that you believe I can render . . .

One sentence from this letter is usually quoted out of context by anti-Nixon writers to "prove" the myth of the 1946 campaign: "I have refrained, for reasons which you will understand, from making any references in this letter to the circumstances of the campaign." But in his book, written in 1947, the complete text of the letter is followed by this paragraph:

A couple of weeks passed and I had received no answer. I began to wonder whether Mr. Nixon had received my letter. Then one day when I came back from lunch he was standing there in the outer office. He smiled and so did I. We shook hands and went into the inner office, which by that time was pretty bleak and bare. We talked for more than an hour and parted, I hope and believe, as personal friends. Mr. Nixon will be a Republican congressman. He will, I imagine, be a conservative one. But I believe he will be a conscientious one. And I know I appreciated his coming to see me very sincerely indeed.

The rise of ground which Pierre L'Enfant selected for the
Capitol is detached both physically and in atmosphere from
the rest of Washington. Even when Congress is in session,
the Hill is placid and quiet. The long stone corridors of the
House and Senate office buildings echo to the passing step.
But Washington is a one-industry town, and beneath the bland
exterior the business of government goes on with guerrilla
ferocity. In his early days of service a young congressman
can be politically sandbagged before he knows what hit him.
He must move slowly, so as not to antagonize the men who
over the years have established a vested interest. If he is too
diffident, he invites oblivion.

When Representative Richard M. Nixon went to Washington, he was neither aggressive nor diffident. He had ideas,
theories, plans—as his early voting record indicates—all fitting
into a pattern, but they had not yet crystallized into what
might be called a philosophy of politics. He wanted to get the
feel of government, to learn how Washington operated, to
discover the pitfalls. And for that he was well equipped. For
he had brought with him one tremendous asset—an overwhelming desire to study and assimilate, to plow through the
mountains of paperwork which are a congressman's lot. He
learned that the work of Congress is done more in committee
and less on the floor of the House or Senate, and he was ready
to attend meetings, listen to testimony, and then take the
record home to ponder. From the start he looked for the tough

assignments, not from any heroic sense but because he realized
that this was the way to learn, and he plunged into them with
characteristic energy. Republican and Democratic colleagues
readily conceded that he was that rare bird, a congressman
who "does his homework."

Nixon had one strike against him. He had defeated Jerry
Voorhis, who was popular with the predominantly liberal
press corps. This was an almost unforgivable sin in the eyes
of many Washington correspondents whose Orwellian view
of the two-party system allowed them to suffer the Republican Party only when it lost elections. The Washington *Post*
quickly tagged Nixon the "greenest congressman in town"
and kept a wary eye on him. That he was green became apparent when he took exception, in the first days, to a pet project put forward by Representative Adolph Sabath, veteran
New Dealer and octogenarian "dean" of the House. Sabath
was agitating for legislation to provide Federal housing for
homeless congressmen. Nixon, who was living with a wife and
baby daughter in one small hotel room, objected. Millions of
Americans were caught in the housing squeeze, he argued, and
it would not be proper for Congress to grab what the average
citizen could not get. He was immediately accused of taking
this stand because he lived in luxury.

Aside from this, Nixon was content to participate in the
work of what President Truman called the "do-nothing"
Eightieth Congress—"do-nothing" because it passed a substantial amount of legislation which Mr. Truman did not like.
Circumstances catapulted him into the thick of the fight over
two controversial measures, the Taft-Hartley Act and the
Subversive Activities Control Act—both of which were passed
over Mr. Truman's veto. The committees which prepared the
legislation were the Labor Committee and the House Un-
American Activities Committee—and in both cases Nixon was
warned that membership in them could defeat him at the polls.

Accepting the Labor Committee assignment did not take
too much soul-searching. For Nixon felt then, as he does now,

that it was equally wrong to consider labor a sacred cow or an ally of the Devil. "Labor is a legitimate force, serving a legitimate function in the nation's economic life," he said. "In every situation its demands and grievances must be judged strictly on the merits of the case. No congressman can do his job properly if he is dogmatically pro- or anti-labor. The same applies to business—big or little. I know this is an unpopular position on labor-management relations, because you catch it from both sides. But it's the only one I can take." Nixon also stressed a distinction. "When you talk about labor," he asked, "what do you mean? There is often a big difference between the interests of the labor leader and the man who pays the dues."

It was the position he took when the House Labor Committee began to write its version of what later became known as the Taft-Hartley Act. Nixon was convinced that the Wagner Act badly needed amending. It had been written specifically to favor the unions at a time when the labor movement was weak. But in the dozen years of its life it had made the unions wealthy and powerful. Some, in fact, had more money in their treasuries than the industries they had unionized were worth. Before John L. Lewis' United Mine Workers could be stopped from literally crippling the economy, the courts had been forced to exact over 2,000,000 dollars in fines—and the union hardly showed any strain in paying them. In the period of the Hitler-Stalin Pact, Communist union leaders had been able to slow down defense production by calling purely political strikes.

There were other abuses. Labor unions could make any charges against an employer, but if he attempted to answer them it was by legal definition an "unfair labor practice." The Constitutional right of *free* association was abrogated, and a worker who did not wish to join a union could be summarily deprived of his right to work. A union member, moreover, had no recourse to arbitrary acts by the leadership; he both put up and shut up.

Obviously the time had come to restore the balance. Representative Fred Hartley, who headed the Labor Committee, took an extreme view of the Wagner Act. He not only hoped to junk most of it but to apply restrictions on unions which would sharply whittle down their power. Nixon took a considerably more moderate view, and since then labor leaders have (privately) thanked him for his efforts. He was interested in the rights of the individual unionist—and the justice of his position became evident after passage of the measure, when the National Labor Relations Board was flooded with cases brought not by management but by union members against their own unions. He was worried about the widespread Communist infiltration in a group of CIO unions. (Some two years later the CIO availed itself fully of the "non-Communist affidavit" provision to rid itself of the Communist monkey on its back.)

On 16 April 1947, Nixon took the floor in the House to debate the opponents of Taft-Hartley. "The issue on this particular legislation," he said, "is that this Congress must recognize that this is the time to enact a labor bill which is not class legislation, but which is in the best interests of all the people of America." And he went on:

> The suggestion has been made that [this bill] was introduced because a few greedy monopolists . . . ordered a bill which would allow them to wring the last dollar out of the laboring men of this country. But what are the facts? When this Congress convened in January of this year it looked back on a record of labor-management strife . . . We know that in the year after VJ-day we had lost $6 billion in the standard of living of America, due to industrial strife. We had seen unprecedented force and violence in labor disputes . . . We had seen . . . how a few persons . . . could paralyze the entire country by ordering a strike by the stroke of a pen . . .
>
> [President Truman] recommended that machinery should be set up providing for peaceful settlement of jurisdictional disputes, secondary boycotts arising out of jurisdictional disputes, and disputes over the interpretation of contracts . . .

I wish to point out that if this Congress were to limit its
action to carrying out the President's recommendations, we
would be acting only on disputes which caused less than five
per cent of the days lost in strikes in the United States in the
past two years . . .

Are the workers of this country, the members of the
unions, objecting to this bill? Or are the objections coming
only from a few entrenched leaders of union labor . . . ? Do
[the workers] object to the fact that the bill gives them the
right to speak freely in their union meetings? Do they object
to the fact that [it] gives them the right to vote freely in
democratic elections for their officers and to organize and
bargain collectively? Do they object to the fact that [it] pro-
tects their right to strike over fundamental issues involving
wages, hours, and working conditions? Do they object to the
fact that this bill provides that where two union leaders are
fighting between themselves . . . such a dispute shall not be
the basis for a strike depriving innocent workers of their
jobs . . . ?

The workers of America have a great stake in the passage
of this bill. It has been said that the public suffers from strikes;
it has been said that management suffers from strikes; but we
must remember that the man who suffers most, the man who
has the greatest stake in industrial peace, is not the public, is
not management, but it is the man who goes out on strike.
[That man] should make the determination as to whether he
should go out. So we have provided that that decision to
strike will be made . . . by secret ballot of a majority of all
employes in the plant affected.

"We passed Taft-Hartley," Nixon says today, "in spite of
all the charges by labor leaders that it would usher in an era
of 'slave labor.' * It's not a perfect act, and I've always said

* This writer, who was employed as publicity director for one of the great
New York garment unions in 1947, recalls a taxicab conversation with a labor
leader, en route to a Madison Square Garden protest rally against the "slave
labor" act. "This is all nonsense," the labor leader said, "all this stuff about
slave labor. As far as I can make out, it won't make much difference to us.
Maybe it'll give our lawyers more work—but they've got a right to a living." He spoke somewhat differently on the platform.

I'd vote to amend it. But it hasn't been repealed because the average union member knows it hasn't hurt his union. And he knows, too, that labor has made great gains, in wages and hours under it—and without paying the terrible price of striking."

Nixon's decision to accept an assignment to the House Un-American Activities Committee was much more difficult to make. The curse of the committee, then under violent and unremitting attack, was mainly that unimportant men had been doing its important work. The careful accumulation of data by the committee staff was often kicked over in undignified political squabbles. Valid material was occasionally put to invalid purpose—and this opened the door to a distortion of the committee's efforts so systematic that to this day many otherwise well-informed Americans believe that it accused Shirley Temple, then a small child, of being a Communist. Nixon's opinion of the committee, he says, was "not particularly friendly."

Pacing up and down in the office of Representative Donald Jackson, a friend and fellow Californian, Nixon debated the problem. "Politically, it can be the kiss of death," he said. Jackson recalls that Nixon "felt the moral obligation to accept, but he asked himself repeatedly if the condemnation of the committee by the liberals was sound; if there were the injustices and irresponsibilities complained of; if the committee could do a sound job." Nixon's Quaker upbringing and his legal training had conditioned him to set a high premium on civil liberties. This may have been a decisive factor in his acceptance of what he has described as "probably the most unpleasant and thankless assignment in the Congress"—he felt that he might be a brake on possible excesses. And he was becoming increasingly aware of the Communist problem and that it would become increasingly vexing to the nation.

It may be coincidence that the most productive years of the Un-American Activities Committee were probably those of

1947 to 1950. The stern repression and social condemnation of anti-Communists, so prevalent during the wartime American-Soviet cobelligerency, had eased slightly. Public opinion had been stirred up by the Kremlin's cold war, the Gouzenko case with its leads into the United States, and the shift in party line among the American comrades. Former Communists now found the courage to step forward, and wavering party members found the strength to break. The committee still had its hair shirt in the person of Representative John Rankin, a Mississippi racist who wandered in and out of hearings asking the kind of irrelevant and inflammatory question which fed the fires of criticism. But Representative Karl E. Mundt and Nixon were there to add stability and direction.

The first witness to appear when the committee began its 1947 hearings was the notorious Gerhart Eisler, a top representative of the Communist International in the United States who had operated here with immunity while living off tax-exempt funds.

"This was really the first time I had brought home to me the character of the Communist Party and the threat which it presented to the country," Nixon recalls. "The Civil Rights Congress, on the very morning that the hearing was held, had circulated all the members of Congress with a petition violently criticizing the chairman for having Eisler subpoenaed. I, of course, at the time did not know that the Civil Rights Congress was a Communist front. I read the petition and was so concerned about it that I went to talk with Bob Stripling and asked him if we were justified in calling Eisler. He gave me a half-hour lesson in Communist activities. I wasn't convinced immediately, but that was the beginning of my education in this field."

At the time he testified, Eisler was in the custody of the Immigration Service, charged with passport fraud. (Eventually he jumped bail and turned up as a Red gauleiter in East Germany.) The colloquy is interesting:

Chief Investigator Robert Stripling: Mr. Gerhart Eisler, take the stand.

Eisler: I am not going to take the stand . . .

The Chairman: Mr. Eisler, will you raise your right hand?

Eisler: No. Before I take the oath——

Stripling: Mr. Chairman——

Eisler: I have the floor now . . .

The Chairman: Just a minute. Will you please be sworn in?

Eisler: You will not swear me in before you hear a few remarks.

The Chairman: No, there will be no remarks.

Eisler: Then there will be no hearing from me.

The committee made several more attempts to persuade Eisler to follow orderly procedure, then voted to cite him for contempt. Before the guards had removed the arrogant witness, Richard Nixon took a long look at the small, balding man, almost mousy in appearance yet strong in the concealed power behind him. Here was a professional Communist revolutionary—a man who had plotted in Germany and China and Spain, who had ordered murders and perhaps committed them, who had practiced every form of deceit and participated in sabotage, and who yet had the temerity to act the injured party before a committee of Congress and defy it.

Several days later Nixon delivered his maiden speech in the House, representing the committee in its formal request for a contempt of Congress citation against Eisler. He was described at the time by Samuel Shaffer, *Newsweek's* perceptive and indefatigable Capitol reporter, as "youthful and intensely sincere" as he delivered a ten-minute speech in "calm, measured tones." Only two congressmen spoke against Nixon—Adam Clayton Powell (who abstained from voting) and the openly pro-Communist Vito Marcantonio (who cast the only vote against the citation).

In the weeks and months that followed, the committee piled up mountains of evidence and millions of words on the Communist Party—basic research on facts which have since become unfortunately too familiar to the country. And Nixon got a thorough grounding on the subject at first hand from the committee's witnesses, as well as from Benjamin Mandel, research director for the committee and one of the real authorities on Communist theory and practice.

Fred Beal, a former Communist who had fled to the Soviet Union after being convicted of complicity in the shooting of a police chief during the strike in Gastonia, North Carolina, told the committee why he preferred an American penitentiary to "freedom" in Russia—and then gave cogent evidence on the Communist forged passport ring.

Ruth Fischer, Eisler's sister, who had been a charter member of the Austrian Communist party and played a leading role in the post-World War I German Communist movement, testified in detail on the conspiratorial and murderous activities of which she had personal knowledge. These experiences and insights she later put into her scholarly work, *Stalin & German Communism*, which was published by Harvard University.

Victor Kravchenko, author of *I Chose Freedom*, testified on the illegal and subversive work of the wartime Soviet Purchasing Commission of which he had been a part before his defection.

FBI director J. Edgar Hoover reported in close detail on the aims, methods, and activities—and the strength—of the American Communist movement.

At the stormy "Hollywood hearings" in the fall of 1947—which could have meant death at the polls for a Californian like Nixon—the extent of Communist infiltration in the movie industry and its staggering financial contributions to the party were sketched in. Great efforts were made by some studios to minimize the investigation, or to laugh it out of court, but the hearings led to a thorough, though temporary, housecleaning.

The investigation of Communist infiltration of labor unions brought agonized howls from union leaders that Nixon and the committee were attempting to smear the American working man and destroy unionism. But Nixon, questioning friendly witnesses as stringently as hostile ones, continued to draw out information which, two years later, the CIO used when it expelled eleven unions as Communist-dominated.

Early in 1948 Richard Nixon was appointed chairman of a House Un-American Activities special subcommittee on Legislation. After a study of the full committee's voluminous hearings, and of two definitive monographs issued during his tenure (*The Communist Party as the Agent of a Foreign Power* and *The Communist Party as an Advocate of Force and Violence*), Nixon's subcommittee issued a report proposing legislation which was later embodied in the Mundt-Nixon bill of that session. The report, written by Nixon himself, ended with these words:

> The subcommittee has not attempted to recommend legislation which will deal with so-called theoretical Communists in the United States. We are seeking rather to strike a body blow at the American cadre of the Soviet-directed Communist conspiracy. We believe that if its criminal activities are prosecuted, its false fronts exposed, and its foreign assistance and direction cut away, the movement in the United States, standing alone for what it is, will be overwhelmingly defeated. We are willing to permit the theories of communism and democracy to clash in the open market place of political ideas in America, but we insist that communism not be allowed to have the unfair advantages in this conflict of the unrestricted use of illegal means, the cloak of secrecy and fraud, and the assistance and direction of a foreign Communist dictatorship.

The legislation which followed, written by Mundt and Nixon, was based on proposals made by a heterogeneous group of liberals and conservatives which included A. A. Berle, Jr., (later to become chairman of the Liberal Party), Donald Richberg, labor lawyer Louis Waldman, Felix Cohen, former Ambassador to Russia Admiral Standley, Dr. William Y. Elliott (professor of government at Harvard), and John Foster Dulles. The bill also had this distinction: it was the first piece of legislation proposed by the committee in the ten years of its existence. And its aim was simple—to force the Communist movement, under penalty of fines and imprisonment, to cut loose from the Communist International, give up its conspiratorial and subversive activities, and become the normal American political party which it has always claimed to be.

Said Nixon in his weekly newsletter to constituents: "Communism, like the weather, is something everybody talked about but did nothing about, but now the analogy ends. The Congress proposes to do something about communism." He was a little previous. Though the House passed the bill 319 to 56, the Senate let it linger on the calendar and then, in the rush to campaign for the 1948 elections, let it die.

When the Democrats took control of the Eighty-first Congress in 1949, the atmosphere had changed sharply. The Hiss Case was at its height, Judith Coplon, a Justice Department employee, was arrested for espionage, and Western European Communist leaders were boldly saying that in case of war between their countries and the Soviet Union they would side with Russia. Mundt (now a senator) and Nixon (who had been re-elected hands down after winning both the Democratic and Republican primaries) reintroduced their Subversive Activities Control Act. But it was a somewhat different bill, snarled up in technicalities and red tape, when the House and Senate had finished amending it.

During the debate, Congress was pelted with mail from opponents of the bill. Nixon examined a large batch of letters and found that though they bore different names, many signatures were in the same handwriting. Other members of Congress began turning up forged communications by the bushel. Some 1500 men and women descended on the capital, invaded the offices of legislators, riffled through mail on the desks, and screamed invective at congressmen. Americans for Democratic

Action agitated against the measure *—and the American Slav Congress sent a passionate protestation which was being broadcast over the Moscow radio at the very moment it arrived in Washington. The bill passed as amended, and today it is wending its weary way through the courts.

In foreign policy the Nixon position emerged fairly rapidly. He believed that the United States had imperative responsibilities abroad, and that those responsibilities were as much to itself as to the rest of the free world. He introduced a resolution, with Representative Charles Kersten, to commit this country to defensive military alliances and to military aid for any free country threatened by Communist infiltration. He appealed for American protection for Trieste and spoke against Acheson's appeasement in the Far East while fighting the Communists in Europe. He favored, in short, a unified American foreign policy on a global scale and a cognizance that the enemy was the Soviet universal state. He did not oppose the United Nations, but he favored the older American internationalism which relied on temporary alliances with like-minded nations and for specific purposes.

In these matters his voice was not merely that of a single freshman congressman. For on arriving in Washington, he had immediately helped organize a potent force on Capitol Hill. Somewhat coyly called the Chowder and Marching Society, it was made up of Nixon and fourteen other freshmen who met regularly, discussed pending legislation and the work of Congress, and arrived at a fairly solid voting partnership. Fifteen votes in a Congress of 435 may not seem like very many. But it was a bloc and a caucus, operating in the welter of conflicting political and sectional interests of the House. As such, it commanded respect well beyond its numerical strength, and it helped give Nixon stature.

When Speaker Joe Martin named the eighteen members of a Select Committee to study the Marshall Plan proposal and to

* ADA chairman Leon Henderson asserted in all seriousness that the Communists secretly favored the Mundt-Nixon bill.

recommend legislation which would convert it into the law
of the land, Nixon was among the ten Republicans chosen.
This appointment, which he learned about by reading of it in
the papers, was one of his most taxing and most rewarding
activities. "It was one of the biggest thrills of my life," he says,
"because I had never been to Europe, and I had never dreamed
that I might be going that year." The group, which became
known as the Herter Committee, after Representative Christian A. Herter, embarked on a strenuous tour of Europe to
determine the needs of eighteen different countries. They
took no dinner clothes, and Nixon announced before they
left: "This will be no junket. It will be no cross-Atlantic
cocktail party." In that month of travel Nixon came face to
face with the misery of postwar life. Against the advice of
diplomatic officials Nixon talked directly to the people. In
Italy he learned what European poverty meant from a Verona
woman who told him that when she and people like her were
without heat, "we go to bed." In Greece he flew to the front,
where Greek troops and Communist guerrillas were still fighting, and talked to soldiers and prisoners. He interviewed not
only government officials—they were always on the agenda—
but also leaders of Western European Communist parties like
Arthur Horner in Britain and De Vittorio, Togliatti's second-
in-command, in Italy.

And he learned perhaps the most important lesson about the
purpose of foreign aid. Speaking of his Greek visit, he said
four years later, "There was no more corrupt or unstable government in the world than the government of Greece, but
we recognized that it was not a question of the Greek government or something better, but a question of the Greek government or something worse, and we gave the Greek
government the assistance which enabled it to defeat the Communists." This lesson, he stressed, was one which the State
Department, splitting hairs over the "corruption" of the
Chinese Nationalists, ignored until it was too late and the
seeds for the Korean war had flowered bloodily.

Nixon returned to Washington with a broader view of world affairs and the firmly shaped conviction that foreign economic and military aid was essential if the collapse and communization of Western Europe were to be prevented. The Herter Committee was lauded for the "staggering volume and intensity" of the work it accomplished, and its report, running to thousands of pages, was the encyclopedic source from which much of the Marshall Plan was derived. He served another and highly important function. He helped influence formerly isolationist members of the House, who respected his judgment where they would have suspected a New Dealer, into supporting the Marshall Plan.

Members of the Herter Committee unanimously give Nixon credit for one Marshall Plan vote they had not expected. Congressman Tom Jenkins of Ohio, a member of the Herter Committee, at their first shipboard conference, proudly informed his associates that he had never in his life voted for foreign aid. He boasted of the fact that he had voted against Lend-Lease and "all those other foolish giveaways." Chairman Herter had assigned Jenkins and Nixon as roommates, probably with Machiavellian intent. At any event, Herter has stated privately that one of the greatest achievements of the group—for which he gives Nixon full credit—was when Tom Jenkins voted for the Marshall Plan and spoke for it on the floor of the House.

Nixon's consistent support of foreign aid stemmed directly from his world view of American security. His votes were down the line on measures for relief assistance to the people of war-devastated countries, for aid to Greece and Turkey, for the Reciprocal Trade Agreements Act, for the Marshall Plan, and for Selective Service—which happened to be all the bills touching on foreign policy which came up that session. Critics have attempted to distort or misrepresent Nixon's foreign policy record—but it is there in black and white, immutable in the archives of Congress. "If anything," Nixon says, "my record here may be too consistent."

The same attempt has been made to distort his domestic record for those years—but with a kind of reverse English. Because Nixon is not doctrinaire, it is hard for the doctrinaire mind to understand how he could vote for all of these: continuation of wartime excise-tax rates, reduction of individual income taxes, removal of disloyal persons from the Executive Branch, abolition of the poll tax, extension of housing and rent controls (and later for the return of rent-control powers to local authorities), return of the tidelands to the states, and admission of displaced persons. The simple fact is that Richard Nixon never believed in repealing the entire New Deal. It was woven into the total fabric of American life, and to junk it would have brought economic dislocation and created chaos. By temperament and conviction he was a free enterpriser. He believed then, and does today, that some of the New Deal was crisis legislation and should be concluded, that some of it needed gradual modification, and that some of it was here to stay. Like Edmund Burke, he believed in tradition as an evolving and organic force. Like Burke, he opposed revolution, no matter how politely Fabian.

As a member of Congress, Nixon made it clear to the voters of his district that he was nobody's man and would vote his own conscience. But unlike his predecessor, Voorhis, who had voted generally with the left wing in Congress and talked conservative when he was in the district, he made it a point always to let them know in what direction that conscience was taking him. He sent out a regular newsletter to his constituents and he broadcast regularly to the district. Once, when he learned of a false claim to "influence" with him, he repudiated the tale on the front page of the local papers. He also instituted the practice of polling his constituents on major issues. Many congressmen poll a select list, but Nixon tried to reach every household in the district, sending out over 100,000 ballots each year. His return on these ballots was over 30 per cent—and the polls stirred up interest in the issues at question, both in the press and at the grass roots. When a poll showed that his district was generally opposed to his views—as in his Marshall Plan stand—on his return home he made it a point to explain his position. His vote on rent control was highly unpopular—the preponderance of voters were small property owners—but the district was willing to give him the right to disagree. "Dick's thinking of the country again instead of us," one apartment house owner said philosophically.

To keep up with his legislative work and to keep thoroughly in touch with his constituents was a considerable strain. Jerry Voorhis had used some of his independent wealth to employ extra staff who provided service for the district. Nixon had to work overtime and on week ends in order to answer his mail and provide the kind of service he felt was needed—and his staff worked with him. The reaction of those he served was best summed up by Mel Rich, city editor of the Whittier paper: "I'm not one of the natives who thinks the sun rises and sets on Dick Nixon, but he is one swell guy. I know lots of people who have disagreed with him, but I've never met anyone here who didn't like him."

The past is prelude. Before his first term had ended, Nixon had made a reputation for himself. Copies of his speech on Taft-Hartley were being distributed in the thousands by other members of Congress. He was known as a speaker who could state the issues simply and clearly. His capacity for work had become something of a by-word in the House Office Building. And his independence was noted and appreciated. Then, in August of 1948, Nixon was put to his greatest test. For on a hot, sticky day, the Hiss Case splattered across the pages of the nation's press. And at that moment the future unfolded.

The Hiss Case represents in dramatic microcosm the trauma of our times. To most Americans it was the struggle of two dedicated men—Alger Hiss and Whittaker Chambers—standing out above the bewildered body politic, a struggle in which truth was confounded and then vindicated in an ordeal by litigation. But to those who looked deeper, and Richard Nixon was among them, the Hiss Case was a signal flashing danger. The basic issue was not Hiss and his perfidies but the fact that they had gone unpunished and ignored for close to a decade.

Had key people entrusted with the nation's security acted in good faith, there would have been no Hiss Case. Alger Hiss would have been dismissed from the government in 1939. Harry Dexter White would never have risen to be Assistant Secretary of the Treasury and the dominant figure in American fiscal policy until 1946. And the Bentley-Golos spy ring would not have shipped bushels of American secrets to the Soviet Union during World War II.

For Nixon, therefore, the Hiss Case has always broken down into two distinct parts. First, there was the question of guilt—summed up in the popular litany of "Who is lying, Hiss or Chambers?"—and the problem of proving that guilt. Secondly, there was the far deadlier question, "Why?" Why had Hiss been allowed to remain in the government? Why had he had been permitted to entrench himself, at 20,000 dollars a year, as president of the Carnegie Endowment for Peace? Why was President Truman so stubbornly committed to the destruction of those who were exposing Hiss? Eventually Richard Nixon found his answers. The full corroboration did not become public until a Republican Attorney General broke open the files of the Justice Department and put the documentation on the record.

It is in the context of President Truman's repeated remark that the Hiss Case was a "red herring"—and of his press conference statement made during the early days of the controversy that no American secret had ever been leaked to the Russians—that the second point assumed its significance. Both assertions stemmed from his inability to separate the Communist problem from partisan politics: hence his angry insistence that the exposure of homegrown traitors was a Republican plot to divert the country from his efforts to reinstitute price controls. The primary result was that Mr. Truman responded to the Hiss Case by issuing an Executive Order barring Federal employees from giving the committees of Congress any information on espionage or subversion—an order issued on the day Hiss first denied Chambers' charges.

The first phase of the Hiss Case was a kaleidoscope of charges and countercharges, shaken into new patterns by each successive revelation. It was set in motion by the testimony of Elizabeth Bentley, a former Communist espionage agent who revealed the personnel and practices of her Washington apparatus in a committee hearing on 31 July 1948. On 3 August, Whittaker Chambers, a senior editor of *Time* magazine, then earning 30,000 dollars a year, took the stand as a subpoenaed witness. He told the House Un-American Activities Committee of an earlier underground Communist cell (most of its alumni were in the Bentley ring) which had operated in the State and Treasury departments. His account was schematic and stressed the policy-muddling and subversion of his group which included Alger Hiss, who had risen to the State Department post of director of the Office of Special Political

Affairs, as well as Harry Dexter White, who had eventually moved from the Treasury to the International Monetary Fund and from Chambers' cell to Miss Bentley's. Espionage was clearly indicated in that first day's testimony.

Committee members had so many questions of varying pertinence to put to Chambers that the hearing at times was like a scattering of buckshot. But with his first question Nixon hit the bull's-eye with a single high-power shot.

> *Nixon:* Mr. Chambers, you indicated that nine years ago you came to Washington and reported to the government authorities concerning the Communists who were in the government.
>
> *Chambers:* Yes.
>
> *Nixon:* To what agency did you make that report?
>
> *Chambers:* . . . I went to see [Assistant Secretary of State] Berle and told him much of what I have been telling you.

Two days later Alger Hiss appeared at his own request to deny every allegation. He was not a Communist, he said categorically, and had never been a Communist. True, all the other men Chambers had named, apart from his brother Donald, were friends or close associates of the time. He did not protest the flat assertion that there was no doubt of their subversive connections. He did not even feel "qualified" to "testify absolutely" that his brother was not a Communist. But he did not think he had ever known a single Communist other than Soviet officials. What's more, Hiss insisted, the Chambers allegation was on the face of it preposterous. He had never known, and here he was very precise in his wording, *a man named Whittaker Chambers.** This, as Nixon later

---

* Chambers' underground alias had been "Carl" and this was the name he used with Hiss. This technique of exact but limited truth adding up to complete falsehood was employed by John Sherman, another witness in the case, who was asked if he had ever been introduced to Hiss by Chambers. His answer was: "I wouldn't know Alger Hiss from Adam." On the face of it this was a denial. The whole truth was that he had, in fact, been introduced to Hiss, and that Hiss had been using the cover name of "Adam."

pointed out, was the mistake that trapped Hiss. For had he acknowledged Chambers as a casual acquaintance of the past, the detailed inquiry to establish a connection between the two men, and the startling evidence which it uncovered, would never have come to light.

When Hiss stepped off the stand, there was a general rush of newspapermen and committee members to shake his hand. The only congressman to absent himself from that felicity was Nixon. He and Robert Stripling, the chief investigator, felt that Hiss' testimony had been a little too "mouthy," a little too careful, for a witness who purported to be telling the whole truth without qualification. They also felt that he had put on a curious performance when he was shown the picture of Chambers. "His elaborate explanation, his statement that 'this might look like you, Mr. Chairman' all combined to make me think that he actually did recognize the picture and was attempting to give a disarming statement concerning it," Nixon says.

The other members of the committee did not share his doubts. Acting Chairman Mundt and the others were certain that the committee had been taken in by Chambers. In executive session, immediately after the Hiss appearance, they discussed what they thought to be their plight, and Representative F. Edward Hébert, a soft-spoken Southerner, insisted that the only way to handle the problem was for the committee to wash its hands of the affair and turn the record over to the Department of Justice. Nixon objected, but he could only plead his intuition. The committee agreed, however, to allow him to pursue the case quietly.

It was Nixon who developed the strategy which brought the Hiss Case to its climax. He reasoned that on the question of membership in the Communist apparatus, it was Hiss' word against Chambers. But he felt that if Chambers had known Hiss intimately for almost four years, evidence of that relationship should somehow be adducible. On 7 August, in a room of the Hotel Commodore in New York City, Nixon and two other members of the committee went into executive session with Chambers. There, for some three hours, Nixon examined and cross-examined his witness exhaustively. Chambers told the committee the nicknames Hiss and his wife called each other, described the homes they had lived in, their hobbies, recalled the location of the kennel they took their pet dog to, and most important of all, the history of an old Ford car. When Hiss had bought a 1936 Plymouth, Chambers testified, he had insisted on giving his old Ford to the Communist party, and the transfer had been effected through a Communist employee of a reputable motor company.

Nixon returned to Washington convinced that he had struck pay dirt. Working on a round-the-clock basis, the committee staff checked the houses were Hiss had lived, searched motor car tranfers and registrations, and even the dog kennels of Georgetown. "The story checked out in every detail where corroborative evidence was available," Nixon said later. "We then concluded that we had enough evidence to call Hiss before us again and ask him to explain how Mr. Chambers could know these things about him."

In the interim the committee had been busy on other aspects of the case. A series of witnesses named by Chambers and Elizabeth Bentley as members of the interlocking Communist apparatus took the stand. Most of them withdrew behind the Fifth Amendment. Some, like William Remington, partially denied the charges.* Victor Perlo, a member of both the Chambers and the Bentley apparatus, read a statement to the committee, denying the testimony against him.

* Remington, an official of the Commerce Department, was cleared by its loyalty board. The committee then produced new witnesses and forced the Justice Department to institute perjury proceedings against him. He was tried and went to prison. The significance of the Remington Case in this account derives from the fact that Americans for Democratic Action set itself up as prime advocate of his "innocence"—and attempted to prove it by mounting one of the first smear campaigns against Nixon, who was active in the case. Arthur Schlesinger, Jr., let fly a rouser by calling Nixon a "junior G-man"—but never bothered to inform his growing public that since 1946 he himself had known the key facts of the Hiss-Chambers Case.

But when he was reminded that he was under oath and subject to the law of perjury, he asked for and received permission to withdraw his statement and plead self-incrimination.

Of considerably greater importance was the appearance of Harry Dexter White before the committee. White, named by both Chambers and Miss Bentley, delivered an address on Americanism, insulted the committee's members, made witty remarks, and airily explained why he had been the biggest single employer (and protector) of Communist agents in the Washington wartime bureaucracy. Having denied everything, he walked out of the room a hero. When, several days later, he died of what the medical records call a heart attack—a doctor other than his own signed the death certificate and he was cremated before any post-mortem could be performed—this was cited as proof positive of his innocence.

On 16 August, the committee returned to Hiss, questioning him behind closed doors. In this hearing Nixon carried most of the questioning—as, in fact, he did throughout most of the inquiry. Taking Hiss over the ground covered with Chambers, Nixon got almost identical answers on every point. As the questioning progressed, Hiss realized that Chambers had given such detailed corroboration of their relationship that it could no longer be brushed aside by blanket denials. He still insisted that he could not recognize the pictures of Chambers which were shown to him, but he began to shift his ground. He "recalled" a man named George Crosley, a free-lance writer, to whom he had sublet his apartment. This Crosley, said Hiss, was a "deadbeat," but he had lent him money, put him up in his home for several nights, driven him to New York, and finally given him his old Ford ("I just turned it over"). All of this had occurred in 1935—a date which assumed tremendous importance. But Hiss did not think, he said, that Crosley was Chambers.

"The obvious thing to do then was to confront these two men," Nixon described it later, "since it was apparent that both men must know each other in view of the testimony we had." The confrontation took place in Room 1400 of the Commodore Hotel.

We brought Mr. Hiss into the room first and seated him in a chair. We then had a committee investigator bring Mr. Chambers into the room and had him sit on a sofa opposite Mr. Hiss. During the time Mr. Chambers was entering the room, Mr. Hiss, who had said he would like to see this man who had made the charges against him, stared straight ahead. He did not turn around once to look at Mr. Chambers as he entered the room. Then we had the two men rise. I said:

"Mr. Hiss, can you identify this man as anybody you have ever known?"

Mr. Hiss said: "I wonder if you could have him speak?"

Chambers spoke. But this did not satisfy Hiss. He insisted that Chambers speak some more. Then he asked to look inside Chambers' mouth while he was speaking. George Crosley, he said, had bad teeth. Nixon asked Chambers if he had ever had work done on his teeth. Chambers said he had.

We thought certainly Mr. Hiss would admit then he had known Mr. Chambers as Crosley. But no. He said:

"I wonder if you could give me the name of the dentist who did the work."

I said: "Do you mean you would have to have a man's dentist tell you just what he did to his teeth in order to identify him as somebody you once knew?" At that point Mr. Hiss changed the subject . . .

For half an hour Hiss fenced with Nixon. Then he admitted that he had known Chambers—as Crosley but not as a Communist. The veneer had begun to crack. At one point he started toward Chambers as if to strike him. He made impossible and illogical accusations against Nixon and the committee. He implied what he had said more baldly to a committee staff member when he was not under oath—that Chambers had been in a mental institution. (This was not true, of course, but Hiss and his friends repeated the story—and others which cannot be printed—to sympathetic newspapermen.)

The private confrontation was followed by a public repetition in Washington. The impact of Hiss' belated admission that he knew Chambers was tremendous. But it was compounded when the true story of Hiss' old Ford was put on the record with documentary proof to back it. For it was shown that one year from the time Hiss had said he forever parted company with "Crosley," the car was still in his possession, that it had never been turned over to Chambers, Crosley, or any free-lance writer, and that in fact—as Chambers had sworn—it had been turned over to a Communist organizer. Hiss' reaction to this evidence was exceedingly silly. He denied what the record of his testimony showed that he had said. This was the beginning of the end. And it had been brought about, as the transcript of the hearings proves, by Nixon's persistence, by his penetrating questions, and by his ability to stay on the subject despite Hiss' artful dodging.

After the second confrontation, the unfolding of the Hiss Case should have been a government matter. It had become clear that Hiss was committing perjury. The Chambers-Bentley testimony had opened up wide areas for an exhaustive inquiry. The State Department had known since 1939 that Hiss was a Communist. The Justice Department had been in possession of Chambers' confession since 1943. Elizabeth Bentley had told her story to the FBI in 1945. But Mr. Truman had left no room for doubt that as long as he was President, the Hiss Case would not be pursued. He continued instead to fulminate against the House Un-American Activities Committee.

Hiss himself lit the fuse which kept the firecrackers popping. At the first confrontation he had challenged Chambers to repeat his charges where they were not privileged, threatening to sue for libel. On 27 August 1948, Chambers said on a television broadcast, "Alger Hiss was a Communist and may be now." When, three weeks later, Hiss had still not taken legal action, even the strongly sympathetic Washington *Post* said editorially, "Mr. Hiss himself has created a situation in which he is obliged to put up or shut up." It took Hiss another week to make up his mind—and then he filed a defamation of character suit in the Baltimore courts, asking 75,000 dollars in damages. Pretrial questioning of Chambers began in mid-November. Immediately Hiss' lawyers began challenging Chambers for documentary proof of his allegations.

On 17 November, Chambers produced four memoranda in Hiss' handwriting, eight pages in Harry Dexter White's writing, and a thick pile of secret State Department documents which had been copied on the Hiss typewriter in 1938. On that same day Alexander Campbell, head of the Justice Department's Criminal Division, was summoned by counsel for both sides. The documents, clear evidence of espionage, were turned over to him, and the principals in the case were sworn to secrecy.

On 1 December, the Washington *Daily News* quoted a Justice Department spokesman who said that the Hiss-Chambers Case was being dropped for lack of evidence. On the same day Jerry Klutz, a Washington columnist, hinted that the Justice Department was sitting on important evidence which could break the case wide open. Nixon was away from Washington, on a cruise, the first vacation for the Nixons since 1946, but two wireless messages reached him. The first, from his administrative assistant Bill Arnold, informed him that there were serious developments in the case. In the second the late Bert Andrews of the *Herald Tribune*, said, "Indications are that Chambers has produced new evidence." From his ship in the Caribbean Nixon sent orders to Chief Investigator Robert Stripling, asking him to investigate, as well as a message to Andrews that he would "reopen hearings if necessary to prevent Justice Department cover-up."

On 2 December, Stripling served Chambers with a subpoena requiring him to deliver any other evidence in his possession to the committee, and Chambers handed over five rolls of microfilm. Enlarged to original size, they gave Stripling a four-foot-high stack of copied State Department documents (the typewriter used, it later developed, was Hiss'), as well as some originals.

That same day knowledge became public that the Justice Department had done nothing about the documentary proof in its possession. Simultaneously there were "informed reports" that the department was planning to indict Chambers, not Hiss.

On 3 December, the Justice Department came to life and Chambers was served with a subpoena to appear before the hastily reconvened grand jury.

On 5 December, Nixon was picked up at sea by a Coast Guard plane and flown back to Washington. He immediately began to light a fire under the Justice Department.

On 6 December, Nixon consulted with Under Secretary of State Sumner Welles and Assistant Secretary John Peurifoy on the nature of the Chambers documents. Both agreed that to publish them, even ten years after they had been copied, might endanger the national security. (To this day one of them remains secret.) That same afternoon Nixon and members of the committee rushed to New York to question Chambers. They were intercepted at the station by representatives of the Justice Department who pleaded with them at a stormy session that no public action be taken. The committee finally agreed, but Nixon warned that new hearings would be held unless the Justice Department acted expeditiously and with probity. That same day the federal grand jury in New York began its deliberations.

On 7 December, the House committee held hearings at which Sumner Welles and Peurifoy forthrightly assessed the importance of the documents in the case and destroyed Hiss' explanations that he had prepared the handwritten memos as part of his work. Both Peurifoy and Welles agreed that the verbatim copies of State Department cables, part of the Hiss-Chambers material, certainly allowed the Russians to break the United States diplomatic code. At a secret session that same day former Assistant Secretary Francis Sayre—Hiss' friend, former employer, and subsequently a character witness in the first trial—admitted that three of the documents could have been taken out of his office by Hiss alone. In the questioning Nixon made another telling point. Referring to the handwritten memos, he asked:

> Did Mr. Hiss [as he claimed] have as one of his duties the paraphrasing of these documents and bringing them back to you in this way?
> *Sayre:* The answer is "No." . . .
> *Nixon:* Do you agree [with press reports quoting "State Department sources"] there was nothing important or nothing wrong with turning this stuff over [to a Soviet apparatus]?
> *Sayre:* I violently disagree, not only because of the substance of these cables, but because some of them were in highly confidential codes . . . [They also] reveal sources from which information was obtained, sources planted in foreign countries . . . You kill off what you have been working on for years.

On 9 December, President Truman again called the Hiss Case a "red herring."

On 10 December, the grand jury prepared to drop its inquiry and to issue an attack on the House Un-American Activities Committee. There was also a new flood of rumors that Chambers would be indicted, which would forever destroy the possibility of prosecuting Hiss. Nixon had been working night and day to prevent a whitewash—"That Richard looked so tired," his mother later remarked, "I thought he would break apart"—and he began preparing for countermeasures. Fortunately the FBI, whose role in the Hiss Case is a classic of crime detection, had also been working ceaselessly.

On 13 December, the bureau came up with evidence of Hiss' guilt so conclusive that it could not be ignored: proof that the documents had been typed on Hiss' Woodstock typewriter, arrived at by a comparison of letters admittedly typed by Mrs. Priscilla Hiss on the same machine.

On 15 December, Hiss was indicted for perjury. Said Representative Mundt, who had worked energetically with Nixon once the true nature of Hiss became apparent, "I hope that nobody anywhere will ever refer to this case again as a red herring." Mr. Truman did.

On 21 January 1950, Alger Hiss was convicted on two counts of perjury involving espionage. The "how" of the Hiss Case had been thoroughly proved in a court of law. The question, "Who is lying—Hiss or Chambers?" had been definitely and irrevocably answered. But the "why" of the case—and its seemingly endless ramifications—remained a dusty skeleton in the Truman Administration's closet. Five days later Richard Nixon stood up in the House of Representatives, having asked for and received a "special order" to discuss the case at length with his colleagues. His speech was the opening gun in a long war. And it doomed him to the unremitting hatred of those who gaze darkly in the blaze of noon.

In the life of Richard Nixon every experience has been absorbed and integrated. So it was with the Hiss Case. He had entered it an investigating congressman who had seen the outer manifestations of the Communist conspiracy. He emerged from it a witness to its subtle power, and a partisan in the anti-Communist fight. What he had comprehended only as a police matter—the treason, espionage, and subversion of the Communists—he now understood as a root evil which sought power not as an end but as a means to remake man in its totally materialistic image. "The treason of the Communists is not against governments but against humanity," he was able to say. His anger was not against Hiss the man, but Hiss the symbol—and this, more than anything else, was what he meant in his outburst to Whittaker Chambers: "If the American people understood the real character of Alger Hiss, they would boil him in oil."

This realization grew out of the facts of the case, the spectacle of the forces which rallied to Hiss' defense, and the smears against himself from perfectly loyal Americans who thought it smart politics to decry the exposure of Communists. But the real catalyst may have been Chambers. Nixon sought him out at first merely to get facts, for these are the lifeblood of the Nixon method. But he remained to offer, and receive, friendship. In *Witness*, Chambers has written:

Throughout the most trying phases of the case, Nixon and his family, and sometimes his parents, were at our farm, encouraging me and comforting my family. My children have caught him lovingly in a nickname. To them, he is always "Nixie," the kind and the good, about whom they will tolerate no nonsense. His somewhat martial Quakerism sometimes amused and always heartened me.

Beyond friendship, there grew up a kind of intellectual kinship which evolved from the interests that he shared with Chambers. Nixon, the political man, had read and reread Tolstoi—both the novels and the philosophical works—and this was a bridge to the universal approach of Chambers and to a person whose richly contemplative mind had brought into focus the problems of man. That Chambers, as writer and editor for ten years, dealt in communication narrowed the span of age and experience.

There is no doubt, then, that the Hiss Case indelibly marked Nixon—as it marked all who were touched by it. But while the actual litigation moved through the courts, Nixon's education in the mechanics of the Communist conspiracy continued. That this aspect of the work done by the House Un-American Activities Committee was only lightly touched by the press is no commentary on its significance. For the facts on atomic espionage in the United States revealed through the committee were more shocking in some respects than the Hiss Case. Day after day Nixon heard personally or read in the transcripts delivered to him, the testimony of suspects, counterintelligence agents from the Manhattan Project, experts, and ordinary citizens who had jeopardized themselves to no avail as willing assistants to the FBI.

There was, for example, the case of Arthur Alexandrovitch Adams, a Soviet spy who had been deported in the 1920's. Adams had returned illegally to this country early in the war years and set up a spy ring which succeeded in stealing atomic secrets from Los Alamos and the Radiation Laboratory of the University of California. The FBI tracked him down, sewed up its case, and was then refused permission by the State Department to make an arrest. The reason given: it would offend the Soviet Union.

Through Adams the FBI picked up the trail of Steve Nelson, a graduate of Moscow's Lenin School of espionage and sabotage whose name was later to wind in and out of the Oppenheimer Case and various court proceedings. The FBI, which put Nelson under thorough surveillance, gathered proof that he was receiving nuclear secrets from an atomic scientist —and observed the transfer of this material to a Soviet Consular official. The case went into the files. Again the State Department had withheld permission to make an arrest.

Security officers of the Manhattan Project discovered that Clarence Hiskey, who had been doing atomic work, was in contact with the Nelson ring. Again an arrest was not permitted. To neutralize him, therefore, they were forced to resort to the stratagem of reactivating Hiskey's ROTC commission and having him sent to Alaska, where he sat out the war in safety. En route, counterintelligence officers searched his belongings and found secret atomic data which he was not authorized to possess. Though he was subject to court-martial, nothing was done.

Lieutenant General Leslie R. Groves, who had headed the entire atom project, capped the atomic espionage hearings with this colloquy:

> *Stripling:* General Groves, did you ever report the efforts of the Russian espionage agents to obtain information regarding atomic development to the President of the United States?
>
> *Groves:* Yes.
>
> *Stripling:* When was that?
>
> *Groves:* It would have to be in 1944. It was contained in a report to the President which President Roosevelt read in my presence and the matter was discussed with me. This was just before he left for Yalta. It was brought to the attention

of President Truman in the first report that was made to
President Truman after he took office, which was as soon as
the Secretary of War could make an appointment, and on
that occasion the written memorandum was read by Mr.
Truman.

Nothing was done about the reports. They were filed
away, victims to the obduracy of men who refused to face
the facts of communism. But for Richard Nixon the evidence
placed on the record by the committee could be neither
lightly received nor easily forgotten. There was a certain
urgency involved, for the same stubbornness was being mani-
fested by the same men while the civil war in China came to a
crisis. President Truman had committed his Administration
to an anti-Nationalist position in the belief that once the dust
had settled in Asia the Chinese Communists would be docile
and friendly—a mistake President Roosevelt had made about
the Russians. Nixon could express his convictions by fighting
the Korean Aid Act of 1949 (and voting against it) until it
included aid to the Chinese Nationalists as well.*

In the field of domestic subversion, however, he had
achieved an expert's rating and could speak up at length and in
detail. While the Hiss Case was before the courts, he charac-
teristically prepared for that eventuality by devoting as much
time as possible to a careful study of the case and its ramifications, to the Canadian Royal Commission Report on the Gouzenko disclosures and their leads into the United States, and
to the question of internal security. As a consequence he was
making himself one of the best-informed men on the Hill
where the Communist problem was concerned. This was a
personal project with him, and one which he discussed with
newspapermen who shared his interest. Once, during a discussion of communism, Nixon suddenly slapped down the
pencil he was holding and exclaimed, "I'll never forget what

* For this he has been flatly accused of opposing aid to Korea. See Chapter VIII.

Steve Nelson answered when we asked him whom he would fight for in a war between this country and the Soviet Union. You know what Nelson said—'I refuse to answer that question on the ground of self-incrimination.' "

More scrupulous than many not to say anything which might influence the court and jury, Nixon withheld his fire until Hiss was convicted. On 26 January 1950, he was free to speak directly to the Congress and to the American people —and to warn that the time had come to turn their backs on the Alger Hisses of the world. He spoke from notes, with the sincerity which comes from intense conviction.

> This case [he said] and the implications which arise from it involve considerations which affect the very security of this republic. This nation cannot afford another Hiss Case. It is essential therefore that we recognize the seriousness of the crime involved, the extent and scope of the conspiracy of which Mr. Hiss was a member, the reasons for failure to bring that conspiracy to light . . . and the positive steps which we can and must take now to guard against such a situation in the future.

Then, in sharp detail, he outlined the background of the case, the events which led up to it, the early testimony and the conflict between Hiss and Chambers. He told of the committee's work, of the obstacles put in its path by the Truman Administration, of the tremendous effort involved in getting the Justice Department to act, giving the story of the case in capsule form. Then he moved on to the aspect which most concerned him. "What is important," he said, "is that we not allow the conflict between these two men to obscure the broader implications of the case . . . In the first place, the conspiracy was amazingly effective . . . The second point we should not forget is that a great number of people other than Mr. Hiss were named by Chambers."

Here he summarized secret (and to this day unpublished) testimony given by Chambers to the committee.

A run-down of the various positions held by the members of the ring indicates the effectiveness with which the conspiracy was able to infiltrate into vital positions, both in government and in industry. Mr. Chambers' contacts included: Four in the State Department; two in the Treasury Department; two in the Bureau of Standards; one in the Aberdeen Arsenal; a man who later became General Counsel of the CIO; one in the Picatinny Arsenal; two in the Electric Boat Company; one in the Remington Rand Company; and one in the Illinois Steel Company. It is significant that the individuals named, almost without exception, held positions of influence where they had access to confidential and secret information. The tragedy of the case is that the great majority of them were American citizens, were graduates of the best colleges and universities.

Then he moved on to the case of Harry Dexter White:

> Since December of 1948, I have had in my possession photostatic copies of eight pages of documents in the handwriting of Mr. White which Mr. Chambers turned over to the Justice Department on November 17, 1948. I had intended to say nothing about these documents, but since Mr. Chambers testified [in court] that he did receive documents from Mr. White, I think the public is entitled to see and consider the evidence.

One excerpt in particular, about a secret agreement to purchase 50,000,000 ounces of silver from China, and the status of China's dollar balance, Nixon singled out for special comment. This information "in the hands of individuals who desired to embarrass the Chinese government would be almost invaluable," Nixon said, citing the opinion of a Treasury expert. The full text, however, was even more damaging. For the White memo was a careful account of the Treasury's most private business, with comments like: "This was done at the President's orders. It remains unknown outside the Treasury . . . Bullitt just called to Secretary (copy not available) comments by Herriot, Blum, Reynaud to him . . . I have heard nothing as to Captain Ingersoll's mission in England beyond my earlier explanation . . ."

Yet, Nixon pointed out, conspirators like Hiss and White and the others remained untouched after Chambers had laid all the facts before Assistant Secretary Berle in 1939 and after he had repeated them to the FBI in 1943. "As far as the individuals named by Chambers were concerned, the only thing that was done to them was to promote each one of them eventually to higher positions of power and influence within the government."

And then he planted a delayed-action bomb—a bomb which exploded in 1953 and should have shattered forever the contention of Nixon's opponents that they, and not he, were the true guardians of the nation's security. Said Nixon:

> Shortly before the first trial of Mr. Hiss, I learned that a secret memorandum, dated November 25, 1945, dealing with Soviet espionage in the United States and prepared by an intelligence agency of this government [the FBI] was circulated among several key government departments and was made available to the President.

Nixon then quoted a paragraph from the memorandum, citing the testimony of Igor Gouzenko, former code clerk in the military intelligence section of the Soviet Union's Ottawa Embassy. Gouzenko warned of a Communist agent in the State Department who was incontrovertibly identifiable as Alger Hiss. "Note the date of this memorandum, November, 1945," Nixon said. It is a date to remember in this account, though Nixon moved quickly to the nub of the argument:

> Why was it that Administration officials persisted in their refusal to act through the years, even when substantial evidence of espionage activities was brought to their attention . . . ? There are some who claim that Administration officials failed to act because they were Communist or pro-Communist. I do not accept this charge as a fair one as applied to the great majority [of officials] . . . What was

happening was that Administration leaders were treating the reports of Communist espionage on a "politics as usual" basis . . . It is customary practice for any administration, be it Republican or Democrat, to resist the disclosure of facts which might be embarrassing to that administration in an election . . . Because they treated Communist infiltration into our American institutions like any ordinary petty political scandal, the Administration officials responsible for this failure to act against the Communist conspiracy rendered the greatest possible disservice to the people of the nation.

This was the crux of Nixon's speech. He continued with specific recommendations for legislation, for changes in loyalty-security standards, and for an "extensive education program which will teach the American people the truth about communism as well as the truth about democracy." And he concluded with one lesson of the case which official Washington has not yet fully learned:

The great lesson which should be learned from the Alger Hiss case is that we are not just dealing with espionage agents who get thirty pieces of silver to obtain the blueprint of a new weapon—the Communists do that too—but this is a far more sinister type of activity, because it permits the enemy to guide and shape our policy; it disarms and dooms our diplomats in advance to defeat before they go to conferences; traitors in the high councils of our own government make sure that the deck is stacked on the Soviet side of the diplomatic table.

America today stands almost alone between communism and the free nations of the world. We owe a solemn duty, not only to our own people but to free peoples everywhere on both sides of the iron curtain, to expose this sinister conspiracy for what it is, to roll back the Red tide which to date has swept everything before it, and to prove to peoples everywhere that the hope of the world lies not in turning toward totalitarian dictatorship but in developing a strong, free, and intelligent democracy.

Nixon's speech, delivered to 150 intent congressmen and a packed press gallery, came the day after Secretary of State Dean Acheson had said, "I do not intend to turn my back on Alger Hiss," in a prepared statement bolstered by a quotation from Scripture. What motivated Acheson to flick his glove in the face of an aroused America remains a mystery locked in his complex mind.* But Acheson's declaration of intention reverberated in the overtones of Nixon's speech and emphasized his theme that the Democrats were playing "politics as usual" with the Communist problem. The next day's newspapers quoted his assertion that the White House had known all about the Chambers-Bentley disclosures long before the House committee made them public. Newspapermen who had hinted about the existence of the 25 November 1945, memorandum now asked openly—and in print—about its contents.

A Scripps-Howard staff writer asked Nixon if he could prove that President Truman had seen the memorandum. "I suggest you ask Mr. Truman," Nixon answered. "I don't shoot unless I have the goods. If the President denies that he saw the memo, you can come back to me for a statement." But, he added with conviction, he was sure Mr. Truman would not deny it. Nixon was right. The White House refused comment. And the quiet throbbed around Mr. Truman, a man certainly not distinguished for taking criticism lying down. But the memorandum was not forgotten. At the request of the Senate Internal Security subcommittee, Nixon turned over an abridged copy to its counsel, Robert Morris, who placed parts of it in the record.

Democratic spokesmen shouted "smear" and "inconclusive"—and they belabored Nixon for not dropping the subject—and for impugning the patriotism of President Truman. This, of course, was the great cry against anyone who pointed

---

* Representative W. Kingland Macy of New York outraged the Democrats when he said on the floor of the House, "Why did Hiss lie and subject himself to perjury charges? I submit that the only logical conclusion is that he lied not to protect himself but to protect others."

out government laxity. Nixon made the careful distinction between laxity and disloyalty—and continued to pound away at
the issue in his 1950 senatorial campaign, as well as in the
1952 Presidential campaign. He was right and he knew it.
The most determined efforts to blacken his reputation, and
the unremitting campaign of falsification and distortion which
filled the liberal press, did not silence him.

Then on 6 November 1953, when the records of government were in Republican control and not subject to Mr. Truman's censorship, the facts began coming out with a rush that
left the country breathless and Nixon completely vindicated.
Speaking before the Executives Club in Chicago, Attorney
General Herbert Brownell reopened the case. "Harry Dexter
White was known to be a Communist spy by the very people
who appointed him to the most sensitive and important position he ever held in government service," he said. This was
evidence of the "persistent *delusion* that communism in the
government of the U. S. was only a red herring," and of the
"*blindness* which afflicted the former Administration in this
matter." (Italics added.)

Democratic National Chairman Stephen Mitchell rose up in
wrath to cry out that Brownell had "tried a former President
of the United States for treason before a luncheon club."
Harry S. Truman followed this piece of hyperbole with the
comment that he had never seen any FBI reports on Harry
White. "As soon as we learned he was disloyal," said Mr.
Truman, "we fired him." But a cloud of witnesses began to
gather, proving that his memory was faulty.

Former Secretary of State James F. Byrnes stepped forward
to say that he had received the report on White, had rushed
to the President to discuss it, and had urged him to withdraw
a pending appointment of White as executive director of the
International Monetary Fund. This conversation had occurred
in February, 1946. Mr. Truman's private reaction to the
Byrnes statement was that "sure he came to see me about
Harry White. But the son of a bitch was more worried about

his boy Alger Hiss." * On a nationwide radio-TV hook-up, Mr. Truman protested his own patriotism—and conceded that he had seen the report.† But he insisted that he had taken no action against White and his coconspirators by agreement with the FBI which, he said, did not want to alert the espionage group. He did not think fit to mention why he had seven times labeled the investigation of Hiss, White, & Co. a "red herring" when he had been familiar with the facts for three years.

The delayed-action bomb of Nixon's 1950 speech exploded. Brownell and a reluctant J. Edgar Hoover (he has always objected to giving public testimony on security matters) appeared before the Senate Internal Security subcommittee. The full story, heavily documented, finally came out. In 1945 and 1946 Mr. Truman had received not one but seven FBI reports—six on the espionage apparatus later outlined publicly by Whittaker Chambers and Elizabeth Bentley in 1948; one exclusively on Harry D. White, listing thirty evaluated and reliable sources to prove that he was a spy.

The FBI, moreover, had advised earnestly *against* allowing White to move into the Monetary Fund because its extraterritorial status would prevent further close surveillance. Mr. Truman had refused to withdraw the appointment: it was already up before Congress and to do so would embarrass his

---

* The implication is unfair. Byrnes was worried about both Hiss and White. And unlike Mr. Truman, he did something about it. On reading the report, Byrnes ordered Hiss to go to the FBI and clear himself. Hiss paid a routine visit to the bureau and then told Byrnes he had received "clearance," which was not true. One month later Hiss resigned in a hurry, aware that his activities were catching up with him.

† Said *Time* magazine: "Men like Franklin Roosevelt and Harry Truman and Dean Acheson knew they were loyal to the U.S.—and knew that 99 per cent of the people knew they were. When charged with softness toward communism, or overconfidence in Stalin's word, or blindness to Communist infiltration of the government, they often reacted as if their patriotism, not their judgment, had been challenged. On a month-to-month basis, this reaction was good politics. But long-range, it kept them caught in the Red-issue flypaper. They would not face the ever-mounting evidence, admit their mistakes, and thus bury the issue."

Administration. He decided to let the appointment go through and then find a way to keep White out of the sensitive post. The search for a "way" was seemingly forgotten, and in May 1946, White was sworn in. The following year he was called to appear before an espionage grand jury sitting in New York. He resigned immediately—and received a warm letter of regret from Harry S. Truman.

Richard Nixon made no public comment on the Brownell-Truman controversy. Privately he said, "When I made the speech I had the facts, and now the whole country knows them. But it would have been better for all of us if Harry Truman had acted on them in 1945 than it is for us to stick him with them now. The only ones who profited by his lack of judgment and his eternal stubbornness were the Communists." He thought for a moment and grinned wryly. "You know, in the '52 campaign Truman said that General Eisenhower and the Republicans had a program of 'anti-Semitism, anti-Catholicism, and anti-foreignism'—and nobody got excited. I guess in politics it's worse to be right than to be wrong. If you're wrong, people forget it. If you're right, they never forgive you."

8. THE NIXON-DOUGLAS DEBATE

It has been said that the Hiss Case made Richard Nixon. This is true in the sense that the depression made Franklin Roosevelt, and false in the sense that the War Between the States made General Grant. For some men, and Grant was one, are cast up to fill a particular role in history, whereas others mold their success though history may accelerate the process. In Nixon's case he had distinguished himself in the House before the Hiss Case gave him a national reputation. Reporters who covered the Hill had already marked him as a "comer," a man bound for the Senate or the governorship. On his side, he had the advantage of geography, for the war years had pushed California into the ranks of the great industrial states from which, by a rule of politics, the kingmakers operate.

The Hiss Case converted the likely into the inevitable. From the time that Alger Hiss' guilt became apparent, there was talk among California Republicans of sending Nixon to the Senate. In a state where three fifths of the voters were registered Democrats, there was a need for a strong candidate. He had to be a man who appealed to voters of both parties and of no party. Behind this need was a quirk of California politics. The Democratic machine had been captured by the left wing in the days when Hollywood was redder than the rose and busting out all over the political scene. As a result, the Democratic bosses nominated those they liked—and often lost elections to conservative or middle-of-the-road Republicans.

Nixon fitted in with the temper of his state. He called himself "a liberal in foreign policy and a conservative in domestic policy"—but the terms were an oversimplification. In neither foreign nor domestic policy did he vote with the extremists. Though he consistently voted for foreign aid, both military and economic, he believed that Congress should retain control of this spending and not allow it to become an indiscriminate outpouring of the nation's wealth. In domestic politics he took a moderate view. On Taft-Hartley, for example, he listened to labor's criticism and voted to amend the act—but he refused to go along with a minority of Congress which sought to kill it outright.

Given his background, his national reputation, and his point of view, he was the best candidate the Republicans could put in the field. The 1950 election seemed auspicious, moreover, and for reasons which had nothing to do with the Hiss Case. A Republican governor sat in Sacramento and was coming up for re-election. The election was for the seat held by Sheridan Downey, a conservative Democrat. As it turned out, Downey decided to retire from the Senate because of ill health, and the aspiring candidates did not have the disadvantage of attempting to unseat an incumbent. The candidate of the Democratic machine was Representative Helen Gahagan Douglas, ex of stage and screen, in many ways a formidable opponent who would enter the campaign with the full aid of the Truman Administration and many of California's labor leaders. But she was vulnerable on the Communist issue, on national security, and on foreign policy, and Nixon felt that he had a fighting chance to defeat her.

On 3 November 1949, Nixon declared his candidacy in Pomona, where he had launched his 1946 Congressional campaign.

> I am convinced beyond question that the election of 1950 will be the most crucial election in our nation's history [he said]. I realize that this has been said before—about other

elections—but we have only to survey the situation here and abroad to confirm this conviction . . .

I am convinced that an even greater threat to our free institutions [than the Communists] is presented by that group of hypocritical and cynical men who, under the guise of providing panaceas for certain social and economic problems in our society, are selling the American birthright for a mess of political pottage. Slowly but surely they are chipping away the freedoms which are essential to the survival of a healthy, strong, and productive nation . . . They are concerned only with the temporary vote-catching appeal of something for nothing. . . . There is only one way we can win. We will put on a fighting, rocking, socking campaign . . .

On the Democratic side, the leading contenders for the nomination were Mrs. Douglas and Manchester Boddy, publisher of the Los Angeles *Daily News*. There was a scattering of other, and minor, candidates, making it a six-way race. All six filed in the Republican primary; five entered the Democratic primary. This cross-filing of Democrats and Republicans, characteristic of California, made for a frustrating and untidy contest. It was conceded, however, that the leading contenders were Richard Nixon and Mrs. Douglas. At the start the issues were national—the record of the Eightieth and Eighty-first Congresses, housing, controls, and welfare-state legislation. But before the June primary voting a series of events took place which shifted the focus of the campaign.

Alger Hiss had been convicted and there was a widespread revulsion to Mr. Truman's red herring and Secretary of State Acheson's nonturnable back. Senator McCarthy had delivered a routine speech on Communists in government, and the Democratic Administration embroiled itself in a war against those who raised that touchy point. Senator Millard Tydings, chairman of a Senate committee set up to study the McCarthy charges, openly stated that he was investigating McCarthy instead. Acheson announced that the Republic of Korea was "outside" America's "defense perimeter"—and North Korea ungallantly took him at his word by launching an invasion of South Korea. Willy-nilly, communism and foreign policy became the key issues in the 1950 senatorial campaign.

The Nixon record and the Douglas record, therefore, assumed prime importance in both the primary fight and the election campaign. And significantly, one of the earliest and strongest attacks on Mrs. Douglas came from the Democrat she hoped to succeed, Senator Downey. Referring to the fact that she had the longest absentee record of any California congressman, Downey said, "She has shown no inclination, in fact no ability, to dig in and do the hard and tedious work required to prepare legislation and push it through Congress." And then he struck where it would hurt the most. "Mrs. Douglas gave comfort to the Soviet tyranny by voting against aid to both Greece and Turkey. She voted against the President in a crisis when he most needed her support and most fully deserved her confidence," he said—and added: "She was one of a small but determined band which fought to the bitter end to keep Henry A. Wallace on the Democratic ticket at the 1944 Democratic convention and . . . she wept in total collapse when Harry Truman was finally nominated over Wallace . . ."

The primary results reflected the opposition of many Democrats to Helen Gahagan Douglas. For though she won the Democratic nomination handily, with 734,842 votes, close to 830,000 votes were cast against her for the four other candidates opposing her on the Democratic line. Nixon polled roughly 20 per cent of the Democratic vote and 64 per cent of the Republican vote. His total in both primaries was more than 170,000 above the combined Douglas vote, but short of a clear majority of the 3,000,000 votes cast for all six candidates. Nixon's attitude, therefore, was as usual one of pessimistic determination. The Douglas forces felt that most of the Democrats who had voted for other candidates would switch over to her, and they predicted that the election was in the bag.*

Helen Douglas, however, was taking no chances. To strengthen her campaign she brought in the big guns of the Truman Administration: Vice President Alben Barkley, Attorney General J. Howard McGrath, Labor Secretary Maurice J. Tobin, Agriculture Secretary Charles Brannan, and the President's foreign aid adviser W. Averell Harriman, as well as Mrs. Franklin D. Roosevelt. It is doubtful that they won her many votes. Californians—calling them "carpetbaggers"—resented the imported talent which, incidentally was at a disadvantage in defending Administration measures which Mrs. Douglas had opposed. Tobin, for example, praised Greek-Turkish aid and said that without it the two countries would have fallen under Soviet domination—and Nixon immediately reminded the voters that he had voted for it and Mrs. Douglas against it.

Nixon, on the other hand, campaigned with the aid of local volunteers for the most part. From the start of the campaign Governor Earl Warren, who was running for re-election against James Roosevelt, said openly that he would not raise a finger for Nixon—and he kept his word. Warren never explained why he had dissociated himself from the rest of the Republican ticket. But it was known that in 1948, when he was the Vice Presidential candidate, he had dissuaded Dewey from raising the Communists-in-government issue. And it was widely believed in California that he did not approve of Nixon's role in anti-Communist activities. On the other hand, Senator William F. Knowland was a vigorous and articulate supporter of Nixon, both in the primary and in the final campaign. Knowland never failed to praise Nixon's role in the Hiss Case in speeches he made all over the state. Warren,

* Even so astute an observer as the San Francisco *Chronicle's* Earl Behrens, dean of California political reporters, told this writer in October, 1950, "This is a very tight race. I think Nixon has a slight edge, but I'm not making any flat predictions."

neither privately nor publicly ever expressed approval of Nixon's part in unmasking Alger Hiss.

Nixon did not have the endorsement of labor, although a number of important union leaders privately gave him their blessing. (The studio unions, which had fought and defeated Communists and racketeers in their ranks, could not violate AFL policy by endorsing Nixon. But their support of Mrs. Douglas was *pro forma* at best.) He did not have union funds at his disposal—or the assistance of UAW-CIO campaign workers from Michigan and Washington to do the thousands of chores which are part of a campaign. He was so limited in funds * that he did most of his campaigning from a Mercury station wagon (when necessary making a few long hops in a plane piloted by a wartime buddy), whereas Mrs. Douglas ranged the state in a helicopter. But he had other assets in the form of Murray Chotiner—rated by experts as among the most brilliant and indefatigable campaign managers in the country, and a near-genius at organization; Pat Nixon, who was always at his side, always smiling and friendly; the embattled Hollywood anti-Communists; and of great strategic importance, the Democrats for Nixon.†

George Creel, President Wilson's wartime information chief and an honored citizen of San Francisco, lent his name and prestige to the Nixon cause. Ruth Turner—former president of the San Francisco League of Women Voters, member

---

* Drew Pearson, with his flair for the preposterous, charged that Nixon had so much money in his campaign fund that he was putting up "Vote for Nixon" billboards in Mexico—a charge seriously repeated by *The New Republic* in 1952.

† The most pointed job done by Democrats for Nixon was to prepare a list of the Communist-front affiliations of Mrs. Douglas: ". . . speaker before the International Workers Order, cited by two Democratic U. S. Attorney Generals as 'Communist and subversive,' . . . sponsor of the Win the Peace Conference . . . cited as 'Communist and subversive' by a Democratic U. S. Attorney General, . . . On October 17, 1947, . . . speaker at a dinner meeting of the Civil Rights Congress, cited as 'Communist and subversive' by the Democratic Attorney General, . . . speaker at a political meeting . . . sponsored by the California Labor School, cited as 'subversive and Communist' by a Democratic U. S. Attorney General, etc."

of the Community Chest—worked as zealously for Nixon as, in past years, she had for President Roosevelt. In a strongly worded public statement addressed to Mrs. Douglas, Miss Turner summarized the arguments of Democrats for Nixon:

> You, and you can't deny it, have earned the praise of Communist and pro-Communist newspapers * for opposing the very things Nixon has stood for. And you have done this, as I and so many of my Democratic friends are well aware, against the judgment and the votes of the majority of Democrats in the Congress.
>
> I am a Democrat and I am an American, and I believe that on the critical issues before the Congress where you went one way and the majority of Democrats and Mr. Nixon the other, they were right and you were wrong.

A Democrat and a woman could strike out with energy against Mrs. Douglas. But for Nixon the problem was complicated by the fact that his opponent could cry foul if he campaigned against her as he would have against a man. "What should I do?" he asked friends. "Should I treat her with kid gloves? She isn't using kid gloves on me." He raised the question publicly in a speech delivered in the early days of the campaign:

> I am confronted with an unusual situation [he said]. My opponent is a woman. There are some whose experience I respect who have strongly advised me that because she is a woman I should raise no questions as to her qualifications for the position she seeks. They say that to criticize a woman might cost the election. I have weighed this problem carefully and have reached a decision.
>
> My opponent *is* a woman. But she is also asking the people of California to send her as their representative to the United States Senate . . . There will be no name-calling, no smears, no misrepresentation in this campaign. *We* do not need to

* The Communist *Daily Worker* had lauded Mrs. Douglas as being one of the "heroes of the Eightieth Congress," while marking Nixon as "the man to beat."

indulge in such tactics. But I say here and now that to the extent that Mrs. Douglas does not reveal, or conceals, her record, I feel that I have an obligation to expose that record to the voters . . .

That record, though never denied by Mrs. Douglas or her supporters, became the basis for anguished outcries that "smear tactics" were being employed against the Democratic candidate. Nixon, however, continued to pound away at the fact that Mrs. Douglas had voted against Greek-Turkish aid; against Selective Service in 1948; with pro-Communist representative Vito Marcantonio 354 times (and often in opposition to the Democratic majority in the House); against appropriations for the House Un-American Activities Committee; against measures to weed Communists out of the Atomic Energy Commission, the State Department, and other sensitive agencies; against citing recalcitrant Communists for contempt of Congress.

Douglas campaign literature had listed among her achievements that she "exposed Communist propaganda in her famous speech, 'My Democratic Credo.'" Nixon quoted from that speech. Its opening sentence was: "I think we all know that communism is no real threat to the democratic institutions of this country." Nixon pointed out that Mrs. Douglas had called for the United States to share its atomic secrets with the Soviet Union, by turning them over to the United Nations, long before the Russians had stolen them and developed A-bombs of its own. She had voted against a bill barring foreign relief to Soviet-dominated countries unless it was supervised by Americans who would see to it that such relief was not used for Communist political purposes.

Mrs. Douglas countered by issuing a "yellow sheet" which accused Nixon of having "joined Marcantonio in voting against aid to Korea." This might have been explosive but for one thing: it wasn't true. In 1949 Nixon had voted for military aid to Korea. In 1950 he had joined a majority of the House in voting down a bill which granted economic aid to Korea, but none to Formosa. When the bill had been rewritten to include both countries, Nixon was among those who helped to pass it.

The "yellow sheet" accused Nixon of having voted to cut foreign aid in half. So he had. Nixon voted with the majority against a two-year aid bill, and in favor of a one-year aid bill with renewal clause. The money to be spent over the one-year period was, naturally, one half of what the two-year bill called for.

Behind the scenes a whispering campaign was launched aimed at totally destroying Nixon. People would ask indignantly, "How can you be for Nixon? Don't you know he's anti-Semitic?" Or, "Don't you know he's Jim Crow?" That his close friend and campaign manager was a Jew did not interfere with the rumors. Nor, for that matter, that he was enthusiastically endorsed by the Los Angeles *Sentinel*, a great Negro newspaper. Nixon's stand on the anti-poll tax bill and on FEPC were brushed aside. "He just did that to look good." So prevalent did these rumors become, that Nixon was forced to issue a statement refuting and rebutting them:

> I have never sought, accepted, or would accept the support of any Fascist or Communist organization [he said]. I have been informed of attempts by my political opponents to create the impression that I have received and accepted the support of Gerald L. K. Smith and his organization. I want to make it clear that I do not want that support [if it is actually being given] and that I repudiate it. Any individual or organization which promotes dissension between racial or religious elements of our population has my unqualified disapproval.

Mrs. Douglas, to this writer's personal knowledge, tried another tactic. "Do you want a good story?" she asked. "Joe McCarthy is going up and down this state campaigning secretly for Nixon. But the Republican press is so ashamed of McCarthy that they don't publish a word about it." When she was asked how anyone could campaign "secretly," she answered, "You just check and you'll see I'm right." The check showed that Senator McCarthy had been in California during the campaign just once, to deliver an anti-Communist speech before a patriotic organization, and had left immediately.*

Despite her own activities in the cause of truth, Mrs. Douglas grew bitter at what she called the Nixon "smear"—though, as previously noted, she could not and did not attempt to deny his recapitulation of her record. Instead she inveighed against Nixon as the tool of the "oil interests" because he supported state control of tidelands oil. Since a majority of Californians favored state control and opposed Mrs. Douglas in her championship of Federal ownership, she was by extension accusing of venality many of the people whose votes she wanted.

As the campaign progressed, she grew increasingly bitter. On several occasions she antagonized labor votes by being acidulous when only a driblet of workers attended her lunch-hour speeches outside of the great industrial plants which fringe Los Angeles. She avoided foreign-policy questions for the most part, insisting that the key issues were social security, unemployment insurance, defeat of Taft-Hartley, and low-cost housing. Why, she asked plaintively, wouldn't Nixon debate her on those things closest to her heart.

This Nixon was both willing and anxious to do, and he let his sentiments be known. The Fresno *Guide* reported her reaction: "More than a month ago," it reported, "the [Junior Chamber of Commerce] invited senatorial [candidates] to debate the campaign issues at one of their meetings. Richard Nixon, the GOP nominee, accepted by return mail. But today, three registered letters later, the Jaycees haven't heard a line from Mrs. Douglas. 'The only thing I can conclude,' concluded President Jack Erbes, 'is that she isn't interested in debating here—but doesn't want to say so publicly.'"

Other organizations had the same experience. Toward the

* Two years later *The New Republic* published the story of McCarthy's "secret" campaign for Nixon as "fact."

end of the campaign the League of Women Voters offered its platform jointly to Nixon and Mrs. Douglas. Nixon was scheduled to speak that night in Sacramento, and declined the invitation with regret. Mrs. Douglas promptly accepted. But there was a sudden change of plans, and Nixon decided to drop in on Mrs. Douglas as she addressed the League. When he walked in, unannounced, Mrs. Douglas quickly finished what she was saying and then abruptly departed. Nixon mounted the platform and "debated" the issues alone.

Nixon's campaign was strenuous enough to tire the reporters who merely had to cover him. Sometimes he delivered as many as fourteen speeches a day—at street corners, clubhouses, auditoriums, meetinghouses, etc., ranging the state from one end to the other. Once, at a big meeting in Los Angeles, Pat Nixon brought 'Tricia, then four and a half, along. She listened with interest as Nixon spoke, then began to grow restive. Finally, during one of his rhetorical pauses, her child's voice rang out loud and clear, "My goodness, Daddy talks a long time, doesn't he." On another occasion, when the whole family was on television, Julie Nixon expressed a similar detachment by probing her little nose contentedly. Later, Nixon remarked philosophically, "Julie honey, you've either just won or just lost me the election."

It wasn't always so *gemütlich*. Sometimes the crowds were small, sometimes hostile. In the industrial areas there were usually a few hecklers who followed the Nixon station wagon from meeting to meeting. Once, outside a factory, Nixon got the silent treatment from the workers eating their lunch. He launched into a discussion of Taft-Hartley, and the men began to drift toward the platform to hear him. Pat began to hand out campaign literature as she always did. "Before he had finished speaking, the crowd had warmed to him," Pat recalls. "He must have impressed them because that locality, usually Democratic, went two-to-one for Dick."

As evidence of how Nixon's support cut across party lines,

there was the cab driver who drew up alongside the Nixon station wagon at a traffic light.

"Are you that Nixon fella?" asked the driver. "Well, I just wanted to wish you luck. This country needs guys like you and Jimmy Roosevelt."

In San Francisco a Douglas sound truck followed the Nixon party, trying to drown him out. It was a cold day, and few stopped to listen. But at one corner, as Nixon spoke, the sound truck began throwing him questions and heckling. The crowd started to grow, attracted by the clamor, and Nixon answered the amplified questions as fast as they came. Pretty soon there were cheers and approval from the audience, and then mutterings of anger at the heckling. People began to shout, "Don't answer them, Dick. Pay no attention."

"I can answer them and I will," said Nixon—and the crowd cheered.

"That sound truck won us a lot of votes in San Francisco," Pat Nixon says. The Douglas forces must have realized this, because from then on the heckling tactics, the pickets, and the attempts to drown Nixon out ceased.

When he spoke of foreign policy, which was most of the time, Nixon stressed the fact that America won wars and lost the peace that followed. He contrasted the Truman Administration's strong stand against communism in Europe and its appeasement in Asia. He demonstrated how this appeasement had led directly to the sanguinary Korean war, and drew his biggest applause when he called for the ouster of Secretary Acheson. He spoke of the Hiss Case, of Harry Dexter White, and of Mr. Truman's red herrings.

The best reply the Douglas supporters could make was to point out Nixon's resemblance to pictures of Andrei Gromyko, thereby creating a kind of guilt by resemblance to the Soviet Deputy Foreign Minister.

Mrs. Douglas handed Nixon one issue ready-made. The Veterans Administration had closed the Birmingham (California) Hospital for paraplegics. For the disabled veterans, this meant transfer to other hospitals far from their families. There was considerable clamor for some action which would rescind the order. In the closing days of the Eighty-first Congress, Nixon had called on the VA to reopen the hospital and had introduced a bill calling for an investigation. Mrs. Douglas, however, promised that she could do better. She was a friend of the President, she said, and she would ask him personally to reopen Birmingham. Not long after she made this vow, she had a conference with Mr. Truman at the White House. Asked if she had taken up the question of the paraplegics with him, "No," she said, "I didn't." That No resounded throughout the campaign.

In mid-October Mrs. Douglas made one desperate attempt to belittle Nixon's role in the Hiss Case. The instrument was Attorney General McGrath, in Los Angeles to campaign for the Democratic candidates. At a press conference McGrath told reporters that "Alger Hiss would have been prosecuted by the Department of Justice" without "prodding" from Nixon and the House Un-American Activities Committee. The author was asked to comment on McGrath's statement. Making it clear that he was "not intruding in a political fight but merely attempting to set the record straight," he prepared an analysis of the Justice Department's actions in the case.* There was no rebuttal from McGrath.

The McGrath ploy was a forlorn hope for Mrs. Douglas, but nobody knew it then. Nixon sustained his pessimism to the very end. On Election Day, Pat Nixon recalls, Dick Nixon firmly refused to listen to returns until late that evening. He decided on a family picnic. "By the time we reached the beach, it was cold and dreary," she has written. "We put up an umbrella and stuck it out for a while, but we were miserable and finally went home." Nixon wanted to go to a movie —and went alone. "As he drove home that night he passed through the Long Beach industrial area, and the streets were

---

* It was a statement running to two pages, briefly outlining what has been discussed at considerably greater length in Chapter VI.

full of sound trucks urging the people to be sure and vote against Nixon. He got home in a despondent mood, sure that we were licked."

Nixon was wrong by over 682,000 votes—the largest plurality of any senatorial candidate that year.

The Senate of the United States has been described as the "world's most exclusive club." It is also the touchiest. For though its caliber may have suffered in the general debasement of contemporary manners and morals, its members have never forgotten that the Founding Fathers meant it to be the councilor of Presidents and the representative of sovereign states. Senators may squabble on the floor, but they are quick to turn on colleagues who overstep the bounds which have been set on debate. Politics may dim the memory of Calhoun, but the Senate likes to believe that under the grime of years it still shines.

The freshman senator, whatever his age and previous condition of servitude, must bear this in mind when he assumes his new and august office. For Richard Nixon, at thirty-eight the youngest Republican member of the Senate, this consideration was of prime importance. The very fact that his reputation was already national complicated the problem, for the Senate is jealous of its prerogatives and suspicious of upstarts. In his early senatorial days Nixon told friends that he was "learning the ropes" and practicing circumspection until he had established himself as a full-fledged member of the club.

Nixon's position as a newcomer was somewhat ameliorated by the gracious resignation of Senator Downey just two weeks after Election Day. This opened the way for Governor Warren to appoint Nixon to Downey's unexpired term six weeks before it was his by election, giving him the advantage over the half-dozen other Republicans who were also elected in November, 1952. Under the Senate's rigid protocol of seniority, the "interim appointment" would give him a leg up on committee assignments. Warren rather abstractedly noted that Nixon was the "people's choice"—and that the short-term appointment would be a "running start."

But the question remained: a running start to what goal? There were three logical committee assignments for Nixon— Foreign Relations, Judiciary (with its Internal Security subcommittee), and Labor. Foreign Relations, of course, would have pleased Nixon. But this was a favored committee, sought after by senators with considerable seniority. There were the same obstacles to any assignment to the powerful Judiciary Committee—even though its subcommittee, ironically, had been set up to watch over the enforcement of a law Nixon had helped to draft. The monumental and impeccably conducted investigation of the Institute of Pacific Relations was in the works already, and in its inquiry into both Communists in government and Far Eastern policy Nixon would have been invaluable.

Nixon was offered and readily accepted assignment to the Senate Labor Committee. The press of senators was not great here. For it was a tough, undramatic, and grueling job, and it left those who did its work open to attack by the unions as an "enemy of labor." The Taft-Hartley Act was still under fire, and most senators shunned the sound and fury of the labor movement's onslaught. Nixon took the assignment though he knew precisely what it might bring. "I'll be sniped at, and worse," he said. "But my work with the House Labor Committee gives me the background for it. Let them snipe away."

Nixon was determined, as he told his friends, not to put himself in a position where he might seem to compete with Senator McCarthy on the Communist issue. He felt, moreover, that there were enough voices in the Senate raised to this point, and his was not needed. Interestingly enough, his most significant assignment came to Nixon through McCarthy. Nixon had been assigned to the Executive Expenditures Committee (since renamed the Government Operations Committee), whose most significant work is done by its Permanent Investigations subcommittee. Its ranking minority member was Joe McCarthy, with Margaret Chase Smith and Karl E. Mundt the other two Republicans. On 25 January 1951, McCarthy invoked his powers as the ranking Republican to remove Mrs. Smith from the Investigations subcommittee and to replace her with Nixon.

McCarthy's motives were mixed. Though he denied that he was retaliating against Mrs. Smith's attacks on him, this was clearly a factor. But he was also genuinely anxious to have Nixon on the subcommittee. Scandals were cropping up almost daily, the subcommittee had almost unlimited authority to inquire into the actions of the Executive Branch, and McCarthy knew that Nixon's "comprehensive background" in investigation would be invaluable. There were cases to be studied, committee sessions to be attended, staff work to be done, complex detail to be absorbed, and meticulous cross-examination to be pressed if the investigations were to get anywhere.

McCarthy was aware of the handicap imposed on the Republicans, a minority on a Democratic committee investigating a Democratic administration. Only by the kind of preparation which Nixon was known to make before every hearing could the Republicans overcome the honest reluctance of Democrats to embarrass their own President. As it worked out, McCarthy threw the fireballs, and it was Nixon's persistent and informed questioning which, in case after case, elicited the information which Congress sought.

There was much to investigate—and much to debate in 1951. The nation was fairly prosperous, but economic gains lagged behind a seemingly runaway inflation. President Truman fulminated against the "special interests" and the Republicans, but in the two years of the Eighty-first Congress, his own party had thoroughly blocked the Fair Deal legislative program. Mr. Truman retaliated by stubbornly undercutting the Congress, and the nation watched the deadlock with a growing sense of frustration. The failure of his foreign policy was apparent, and the corruption of his "government by crony" was becoming an international scandal. The first enthusiasm over Mr. Truman's courageous action in Korea had been soured by disclosures that the United States was unprepared for war—and that the vast outlays of money for defense had been badly spent.

The Republicans were not laggard in pointing this out to the nation. The "do-nothing" Eightieth Congress had set the strength of the armed services at over 2,000,000 men, only to have President Truman reduce it to 1.4 million—despite the increasing commitments of the Truman Doctrine and NATO. The Republican Congress had voted a 70-group Air Force and appropriated the money to create it. But Mr. Truman had impounded well over one billion dollars earmarked for the Air Force and had ordered that it be maintained at only forty-eight groups. As a result the Korean war found the armed services short of men, short of planes, and short of ammunition.

Far Eastern policy was still being made by the same group of willful men who had insisted that the Chinese Reds were "agrarian reformers"—and who had sent General Marshall to China to force a coalition between the Nationalists and the Communists. It was being asked why General Marshall, as he put it, had embargoed all military supplies to the Nationalists "with the stroke of a pen," at a time when they were desperately engaged on the Chinese mainland; why millions in aid to Formosa had been withheld; why other millions in aid to Korea had been shortstopped so that in over two years it had consisted of no more than a couple of hundred dollars' worth of barbed wire. The Administration had sought valiantly to sweep this issue under the rug—along with the Communists-in-government issue—but the lumps showed.

On the national scene, "natural royal pastel mink" and "deep freezer" had become symbols of widespread "influence peddling" in the Administration. The President had stuck loyally to General Harry Vaughan and to others in his official family, but the long green herring continued to flap on the White House lawn. When outright fraud and corruption in the Internal Revenue Bureau and the Reconstruction Finance Corporation were revealed, tax-scarred Americans could not take it lightly—and Republicans reminded them of the Kansas City vote frauds and Mr. Truman's persistent loyalty to the Prendergast machine.

Corruption in government and the Korean war were therefore to occupy most of Richard Nixon's attention in the Eighty-second Congress. He had stressed both issues during his election campaign, and he returned to foreign policy in a speech before the Women's National Republican Club on 27 February 1951. Though he had been among the first to applaud President Truman for committing American forces to Korea,* he was unwilling to sit by and watch the State Department interfere in tactical military decisions. He was also angry and distressed by the halfhearted support which the United Nations was giving this country.

In his speech to the Republican women Nixon strongly attacked the Achesonian policies in the Far East which had, willy-nilly, brought on the war. He ridiculed the State Department's ambivalent attitude toward communism, and pointed out that even after the North Korean invasion it was still reluctant to bolster the defenses of Formosa or to encourage anti-Communist guerrilla activities on the Asiatic mainland. He called for full participation in the conflict by the UN,

* Contrary to the charge that he refers to it as "Truman's war"—a slogan actually coined by the late Senator Kenneth Wherry.

for a UN resolution branding Red China the aggressor, and
for a UN embargo on China. Trade with the Chinese Communists, which amounted then to over one billion dollars
annually, should be cut off, Nixon insisted—he found it shame-
ful that "we are fighting Communists in Korea and feeding
them through Hong Kong." He agreed that "unity" was essential, but he warned that "unity on a policy that is wrong
can bring disaster."

Less than two weeks later, on 11 April, President Truman
answered his critics by removing General MacArthur from his
command and ordering him to return home. The national reaction was immediate and spontaneous. Congress was swamped
by over 100,000 telegrams—Nixon alone received some 7000—
and the number of letters was even greater. The Post Office
and Western Union said they had never seen anything like it.
In California Mr. Truman was burned in effigy, and long-
shoremen in New York walked off the job. Nixon was shocked
by MacArthur's recall, though he never questioned the President's authority to fire a general. He hoped, however, that
the Great Debate on foreign policy set off by the MacArthur
Incident would force the Truman Administration to recon-
sider its suicidal China policy and lead to a new and more
salutary position.

Though he was not a member of the Joint Senate Committee which heard MacArthur and a series of Administration
witnesses *in camera*, he attended many of the MacArthur
hearings and gave himself the task of describing and explaining what the public knew about only through carefully cen-
sored transcripts. Millions of words of the expurgated testimony were published faithfully by the New York *Times*
—but few other newspapers had the space or the inclination
to follow suit—so there was a great deal of explaining to be
done. In a series of speeches—here synthesized—Nixon gave a
picture of MacArthur and his own views on the issues involved, and incidentally revealed some of the professional atti-

tudes of an experienced interrogator toward the witness. He told his audiences:

> . . . The members of the Senate who sat and heard him for those three days were impressed by the sheer physical endurance of the man. Anyone who for seven, eight, and nine hours a day could sit there and answer questions as he did would be a remarkable man. And General MacArthur is seventy-one years old. In addition to the physical endurance which he displayed, it was a tremendous intellectual performance. Even General MacArthur's critics will agree that he is one of the ablest men of our times, a man with rare intellectual ability. Throughout the three-day period, not once did General MacArthur come into the hearing room with a file full of papers; not once did he ask to refer to documents before answering a question.
>
> The technique he displayed was extraordinary. Senator McMahon had been briefed well by the Administration and had prepared a number of very good questions, but he made a fatal error in cross-examination. He telegraphed his punches. He adopted an antagonistic attitude toward the witness. The result was that General MacArthur sensed the motive of virtually every question. Time after time he would sit back in the witness chair and say, "Well, now, Senator, the implication of that question as I understand it is . . ."
>
> A considerable amount of tension had built up in the hearing room. Senator Fulbright, with that soft Arkansas drawl of his, started his questions along this line: "General, I want to make the record clear on one point. Certain misinformed representatives in the Senate and the Congress have referred to Wisconsin as your native state. Now, General, for the record, I want you to state here in a positive manner where you were born."
>
> General MacArthur smiled and said, "Well, Senator, I was born in Little Rock barracks in Arkansas, and I remember that one of the early jokes with which I was twitted was the comment that I was born when my parents were away." You can see that the tension which had been built up by the previous questioners was completely dissipated and from then

on, we saw a real battle between an able cross-examiner on
the one hand and an able witness on the other.

General MacArthur had developed a special technique to
handle [difficult] situations . . . Whenever a very difficult
question was asked, like: 'Do you think war is inevitable?' this
is what General MacArthur would do. He would take his
pipe from between his teeth, pick up a match and scrape out
the ashes, knock out the bowl in the ash tray, put in some
Prince Albert from a tin which was beside him, put the pipe
back between his teeth, light it, and then answer the question. In that way he got the time he needed to think and
nobody could be sure that he wasn't just lighting his pipe.

Now enough of the background. What does the Mac-
Arthur incident mean, you may ask. All the wires, the letters,
the tremendous emotional reaction of the people: does it
mean that the country is for MacArthur's program? I think
that in all fairness we will have to recognize that a great deal
of the reaction was not so much pro-MacArthur as anti-
Administration.

Then Nixon sketched in the causes for anti-Administration
feeling: the loss of China and the betrayal of Chiang Kai-shek,
so shabbily rationalized in the State Department's White Paper; the public announcement by Secretary Acheson that
Korea was not a military concern of this country; the clear
antagonism to strengthening anti-Communist forces in Asia;
the weakness of Far Eastern policy. "At the conclusion of the
most costly war in the nation's history we were the most
powerful nation on the face of the globe and had a monopoly
on the atomic bomb," Nixon said.

Five years have passed since then, five years of conferences
and little wars. Today we no longer are stronger than the
enemy on the ground; we are stronger in strategic air, but
not as strong in tactical air. We are stronger on the sea, but
weaker under the sea. And they have the atomic bomb. Five
years ago the odds in people in the world were nine to one in
our favor. Today they are five to three against us.

The conduct of the war in Korea was another step in the nation's five-year retreat, Nixon said. And only immediate and energetic action could bring victory in a conflict which had already been thoroughly compromised by political tinkering. He predicted that a continuing stalemate would force the United States eventually to accept half-victory, which meant whole defeat in the propaganda war but which would become inevitable. As of that date, however, Nixon could see three possible ways to end the war: (1) an abject withdrawal from Korea, (2) a political settlement with the Reds, and (3) a complete victory on the battlefield. The first way was out of the question; the second would mean that we would be forced to "compromise" by giving the Chinese Communists a seat in the United Nations and surrender control of Formosa.*

> This means [Nixon said] that the only way we can end the war in Korea is to win it on the battlefield. General MacArthur was fired because he suggested steps which he said could and should be taken to bring military victory on the battlefield. But Secretary Acheson and the Administration in opposing the steps General MacArthur recommends have consistently failed to offer any alternative program of their own. The Administration policy adds up to this: They will continue the war as it is until the Communists somehow, some time in the future, see the light and quit.

Hopefully, Nixon pointed out what seemed then like an Administration change of heart. General Marshall, in his testimony before the Joint Senate Committee had categorically stated that Formosa was essential to our defenses. The Senate had attached a rider to an appropriations bill, denying foreign-aid funds to any nation which continued to ship strategic materials to Red China. And the American commanders in Korea had been given authority to bomb Manchurian bases

---

* There were already some within the Administration who suggested quietly that such a "compromise" would be beneficial to the United States because it would allow the Chinese Reds to "save face" and thereby drop their aggressive policies. Mao Tse-tung will be another Tito, they said.

in the event of massive Communist air attacks. This, Nixon said, was a beginning, but it was not enough. He outlined additional steps to be taken:

> Secretary Acheson and the President should follow the lead of General Marshall and make a forthright unequivocal statement that Formosa is essential to our defenses . . . and that the United States will use the veto to keep Red China out of the United Nations.
>
> We should warn the Chinese Communists that, unless they cease their aggression against Korea by a certain date, our commanders in the field will be given the authority to bomb Manchurian bases.
>
> We should take the required steps, including naval blockade if necessary, to stop all trade with Communist China.
>
> We must develop as many allies as possible in Europe and Asia.
>
> We must, as we defend ourselves militarily against our enemies abroad, declare war on waste and inefficiency at home. Otherwise, we may spend ourselves into bankruptcy—as Marx, Lenin, and Stalin predicted.
>
> We should recognize that one of the greatest assets on our side in the present struggle are the millions of people behind the Iron Curtain who are not Communists. We should quit talking about containment and defense and go on the offensive in the ideological struggle. The Voice of America is not competent to handle this assignment. The whole program should be taken out of the State Department and set up as a separate agency similar to ECA. The amount of funds appropriated for this purpose should be at least equal to what the Communists spend.

Nixon believed firmly that actions such as he proposed would end the Korean bloodletting in victory for the United States. Whether he was right is one of history's if-Booth-had-missed questions—although subsequent events tend to show that if it had taken strong action in 1951 the Truman Administration would not have had to submit the nation to the long Korean negotiations which allowed the Communists to dig in so thoroughly that only all-out war could have blasted them out. Certainly, no one can deny that the war was lost during the two years of futile debate at Kaesong, nor can it be gainsaid that the failure of the negotiations forced President Eisenhower to salvage what he could from a ghastly situation by agreeing to a truce.

It can be demonstrated that Senator Nixon's hopes for an Administration change of heart were illusory. For once the Great Debate had petered out in the bickerings of the Joint Senate Committee over what the MacArthur hearings meant, the excitement over foreign policy subsided—and the nation moved on to other, newer topics. In July 1951, the spotlight shifted to another scandal in the Truman Administration, reaching high into the councils of the Democratic Party. For Mr. Truman it was a case of changing petards in midstream— but the shift must have been a relief. This was something he could understand.

The first break in the scandal came when the St. Louis *Post-Dispatch*, a Fair Deal newspaper which had devoted itself tenaciously to exposing Fair Deal corruption, charged that Democratic National Chairman William M. Boyle, Jr., and Internal Revenue Collector James P. Finnegan had used political pressure to secure an RFC loan for the American Lithofold Corporation of St. Louis. Boyle denied the accusation. "I had nothing to do with the granting of the loan," he said. But it couldn't stop there. Boyle was one of the President's oldest and closest friends, Senator Truman's secretary, the top strategist in the 1948 campaign, and a key man in the Democratic hierarchy. Senator Clyde R. Hoey, the courtly and conscientious Democratic chairman of the Senate Permanent Investigating subcommittee, instituted hearings on the charges, if only for the protection of his party.

From the start of the hearings on Boyle, Nixon bore down with the same tenacity and careful preparation that had marked his cross-examination in the Hiss Case. From early testimony by Lithofold witnesses it was learned that the company had three times been turned down for loans by the RFC's St. Louis office and by the RFC's Board of Review. Then Boyle had been retained at 500 dollars a month, although he was already acting chairman of the Democratic National Committee. Boyle called up an RFC official, made an appointment for two members of the Lithofold Company—and a loan of 565,000 dollars was granted in short order.

The case developed rapidly and sensationally. The subcommittee learned that Boyle had received over 100,000 dollars from Max Siskind, his former legal associate, as payment for turning over a number of lucrative cases involving the government. Nixon immediately asked that Boyle's income-tax returns be submitted to the committee, and he demanded that Boyle and Siskind be subpoenaed. When Siskind appeared, he insisted that he had bound himself to pay Boyle 150,000 dollars as "forwarding fees" for twenty-three pending cases, but that he had paid nothing for the Lithofold account. Under sharp questioning he submitted a list of those pending cases. They included another RFC loan—also granted—as well as cases before government agencies. Forty per cent of them, Nixon brought out in questioning, had been handled by Boyle while he was acting Democratic chairman.

"I severed all relations with my practice when I came to Washington," Nixon told Siskind.

"Just like Mr. Boyle," Siskind answered.

"Except for the 150,000 dollars," Nixon shot back.

It was a perfectly legitimate transaction, Siskind insisted. But he could not explain why the 150,000-dollar deal had never been put in writing or why an employee of Lithofold had been ordered to carry the monthly statements of payments to Boyle and Siskind on the books as "salesmen's commission"—and told to keep vouchers face down on her desk, after Boyle became National Chairman, so that no else could see them. Siskind had no answers to these questions. It remained for Chairman Boyle to explain.

On the witness stand, however, Boyle described himself as a man utterly devoid of influence in Washington, insisted that he had done nothing "improper," and added that in calling the RFC he was doing his duty as an official of the Democratic Party—a statement with which the Republican members of the subcommittee could wryly concur. His call to the RFC, in behalf of Lithofold, had been routine. After becoming Democratic National Chairman he had stopped practicing law. Nixon recalled that the Lithofold loan had not been granted until Boyle's intervention.

"As a result of the call—the facts speak for themselves—Lithofold got the loan," Nixon said. "How can you sit there and tell us you had no influence and that a call from Bill Boyle, acting chairman of the Democratic National Committee, meant no more than a call from anyone else?"

"Senator, you are presuming quite a lot," Boyle protested, "to think that a telephone appointment for someone would get some kind of a loan in government."

"I know that my telephone calls do not do that," Nixon said. "That is why I am curious about yours. Tell me about the ones of yours that were turned down for your clients."

"Well . . . ," Boyle hesitated.

"Name them, all of them, if you will."

Boyle shrugged. "I have not a record of my clients," he said.

And then, several days later, Nixon presented some startling new evidence to the subcommittee. Boyle, he noted, had kept H. Turney Gratz, an RFC employee, on his own payroll for four years, paying him 11,000 dollars. According to Boyle's income-tax returns, payments to Gratz had been "fees for services and reports" and "reimbursements to employees, agents, and representatives." Gratz described his services as "overtime work" in the evenings on Boyle's investments and personal accounts. This did not satisfy Nixon. In the diary of an RFC director he found that Gratz had arranged at least one appointment for Siskind at the RFC.

Shortly thereafter, Boyle resigned as Democratic chairman, giving ill health as his reason. But the subcommittee had moved on to another inquiry. A study of RFC records had shown that Guy G. Gabrielson, the Republican National Chairman, had applied for and received loans from the RFC for a company in which he had a financial interest. A number of Republican senators came to his defense on the ground that he could exert no influence during a Democratic Administration. But Nixon, who had already called for Boyle's resignation, could not see why a double standard should apply. Though he conceded that there was no "moral turpitude" involved in either case, he felt that Gabrielson too should resign—a stand which considerably irritated some of Nixon's fellow Republicans.

"Regardless of the merits of Mr. Gabrielson's position and regardless of how many times he reiterates his innocence of any wrongdoing, his effectiveness as chairman of the minority party has been irreparably damaged," Nixon said. "While it is true that the Republican National Chairman has less influence than the Democratic National Chairman, it must be remembered that he has the power of criticism and the potential power of recommending appointments."

But the RFC pot continued to boil merrily. It was discovered that Mrs. Flo Bratton, Vice President Barkley's secretary for more than twenty-five years, had presented herself to the RFC to intercede in behalf of a friend who needed 1,100,000 dollars to build a hotel in Miami Beach. She was accompanied by Charles E. Shaver, another government official. Although the RFC had already rejected the proposition four times, it reversed itself for Mrs. Bratton. Said Nixon, "Staff investigation has shown some substantial bank deposits by Shaver which will have to be explained." Shaver, who had been counsel to the Senate Small Business Committee, resigned; but Mrs. Bratton protested, "I don't call it influence when you just inquire about the status of a loan application.

I never got anything . . . no money, no trips, no fur coats, no nothing." *

As the cases—and the scandals—piled up, President Truman finally promised to take "drastic action." This, it turned out, was the appointment by Attorney General McGrath of Newbold Morris, a pleasant though ineffectual New Deal Republican, to clean up the mess in Washington. "He's too little and McGrath is too late," Nixon remarked. There was an element of the incongruous in the appointment of Morris, moreover, for he was himself under investigation by the Executive Expenditures subcommittee for his role in some highly dubious oil-tanker transactions—deals complicated by the fact that some of the tankers, bought as surplus from the government, had been running oil to Red China.

Morris' part in the whole affair was innocent; he was head of a foundation which owned all the stock in a corporation operating the tankers, but he knew nothing about the matter until the subcommittee called it to his attention. When he was called before the subcommittee, Morris lashed out at the "diseased minds" and the "mental brutality" of his questioners—and then called a press conference at which he threatened to tour the country lecturing on the iniquities of Congress. His performance—and what Nixon called his "violent, childish outbursts" and "basic emotional instability" —destroyed whatever chances of cleaning house Morris may have had. Eventually he was fired by McGrath, who was fired in turn by Mr. Truman.

Scandals continued to pop until well into 1952—and Nixon tried in vain to get some cooperation from Mr. Truman and the Executive Branch in investigating them. But the record had been made, and again the national attention shifted. The average citizen was convinced that the "mess" existed. He was interested now in the upcoming Presidential campaign,

* "You know how Flo is," said Barkley. "She's got a heart as big as all outdoors, and friends all over the country. The charitable view is that she just couldn't resist a chance to help somebody."

the primary fights, the conventions, and the ordeal by ballot which faced the candidates—whoever they might be. As a member of the Senate—and as a leader of his party in California, and a delegate to the nominating convention—Richard Nixon had a stake in the quadrennial game of choosing up sides. He had no way of knowing, however, how big the stake would become.

The year 1952 began with a particular excitement. A Presidential election was in the making, and it was a time of decision for the Republican Party and the Democratic Party. The Republicans, who had been so tantalizingly close to victory in 1948, felt that it was now or never. After twenty years out of power, only the most doughty could face the bleakness of another Democratic victory. The Democrats were divided, bitter, at odds with a President whose popularity sank ever lower in the polls, and lacking a candidate.

The Republicans had, unfortunately, two candidates. Both were men of great stature; both had zealous followers who loudly asserted that they would brook no compromise. On the one hand, Senator Robert A. Taft represented a policy of moderate conservatism—and the organizational core of Republicans who had held tenaciously to their faith through the lean years. On the other, General Eisenhower represented a policy of moderate liberalism—and the rich, powerful, and highly pragmatic Dewey wing of the Grand Old Party. Richard Nixon was, from the start of the pre-convention struggle, a bridge between the two groups. The charge that he was a "reactionary"—whatever that means—had not yet reached the public prints or the public consciousness. Liberal Republican newspapers like the New York *Herald Tribune* classified him among the party's liberals. The Taft, or conservative, wing respected Nixon for his uncompromisingly anti-Communist record, his undoctrinaire position on Taft-Hartley, and his commitment to the free enterprise system.

Nixon's voting record in the Eighty-second Congress is an index to the confidence which both wings of the Republican Party were ready to place in him. It was a record of moderation, achieved before moderation became a slogan for the immoderate. He was recorded in this manner on these measures:

> Against the Kem amendment to the UMT bill barring ground forces in Europe without certification by the Joint Chiefs of Staff that there was available air power to secure their effectiveness.
>
> For a McCarthy amendment that the resources of West Germany, Spain, Turkey, and Greece be utilized on a voluntary basis in the defense of Europe.
>
> Against a Wayne Morse amendment to the Defense Production bill suspending price supports on agricultural commodities.
>
> Against a Ferguson amendment raising ceiling prices.
>
> Against a Paul Douglas measure which sought to cut down funds for the Bureau of Reclamation.
>
> Against a Douglas attempt to cut down foreign service allowances and reduce funds for the acquisition of buildings abroad by the State Department.
>
> For the Mundt amendment which increased funds for informational and educational activities abroad. (Voice of America, libraries, etc.)
>
> Against attempts by Dirksen to cut 500 million dollars from ECA funds, by Long to cut 250 million dollars, by Dirksen to cut 250 million dollars from military aid, for Benton amendment to discourage cartel practices and encourage the growth of free labor unions, for a compromise token cut of 39 million dollars from ECA—and for passage of the bill.
>
> Against a Douglas measure to make it a felony knowingly to employ illegal aliens.

Both wings of the party, moreover, were grateful to Nixon for the aid he had given Joseph Holt in the 1952 California

Congressional primaries. Holt was running against State Senator Jack Tenney, who had accepted the support of Gerald L. K. Smith. By helping Holt defeat Tenney for the Republican nomination, Nixon did not merely express his own convictions but also nullified further demagogic attacks, such as those launched by Senator Herbert H. Lehman and other Democrats, that the party tolerated anti-Semitism. During the 1952 Presidential campaign, when charges were rife that both Mr. Eisenhower and Nixon were anti-Semites, the Anti-Defamation League of B'nai B'rith cited the Holt-Tenney episode—along with other anti-racist acts—in its defense of the Republican standard bearers.

Nixon was able to move into the first stages of the 1952 campaign with no entangling alliances. He could therefore caution both camps of the Republican Party against letting pre-convention passions run too high. On 19 February 1952, he repeated earlier warnings in specific and energetic terms. "The greatest threat to Republican victory in November," he said, "is being created by what Republicans themselves, rather than Democrats, are doing and saying. Though the major candidates have themselves avoided personalities in their campaign to date, their supporters are saying things now which will be used to defeat the man who may be selected as the Republican candidate in July. Too many people today are declaring that if their candidate fails to get the nomination they are going to 'take a walk.' What all of us must bear in mind is that our major objective is to defeat the present Administration."

His own views on who the candidate should be, however, were no secret. Early in 1952, at a small gathering of friends, Nixon explained his position. "I have tremendous respect for Bob Taft," he said. "I like him personally and I think he would make a fine President. I've met Eisenhower twice, and I found him to be tremendously impressive. But I think it narrows down to this. I don't say Taft can't win, but I do say that I'm not *sure* he can win. And I'm sure Eisenhower can win. If I thought Eisenhower were the wrong man for the job, none of this would make any difference. But I think he'll make a fine President—and I think the Republican Party has to win, if only to clean up the mess in Washington."

Senator Taft and his associates were aware of Nixon's sentiments. They could disapprove—but that was as far as their criticism could or did go. For Nixon, however, and for other California Republicans, the Taft-Eisenhower conflict was complicated by an additional factor. Governor Earl Warren suddenly decided to make a try for the nomination. He had been unable to carry California when he ran with Dewey in 1948, but he nevertheless declared himself a favorite son. Though he publicly announced, when entering the Wisconsin primary in April, that he would release his delegates to Mr. Eisenhower if he saw that he had no chance at the convention, he was soundly defeated by Taft. The Wisconsin vote put him out of the running, but Warren clung to the somewhat whimsical hope that lightning might strike if the convention were deadlocked. As a result, he ran in the California primaries, winning the state's seventy-six convention votes. Under California law the delegates were pledged to him until such a time as he might release them.

Shortly after the California primary Nixon decided that it was of some importance to determine where his constituents stood on the main contenders. Reviving his old practice of polling the voters, he sent out some 25,000 letters. "As a result of the primary election of June 3," he wrote, "I am to be one of the delegates to the Republican National Convention. This delegation is pledged to support Governor Warren for President." Reminding his constituents that Warren had promised to release his delegation, should he fail to make it, he asked them to fill out the blank in the following statement: "From my conversations with other voters and my analysis of all the factors involved, I believe that ——— is the strongest candidate the Republicans could nominate for President." The vote was overwhelmingly for General Eisenhower.

Nixon did not release the results of the poll. But it reassured him that his espousal of the Eisenhower cause reflected more than his personal views. He continued to deplore attacks on Senator Taft made by some of the more enthusiastic Republicans on the Eisenhower side, striving to maintain party unity, but he made his own sentiments on the choice of a candidate abundantly clear. Equally clear was the fact that his relations with Warren were correct—and not much more. He did not say it—but friends pointed out that, given Warren's behavior in 1950, Nixon owed him no political loyalty. (Those with longer memories recalled that in 1946 Warren had refused, despite the urging of many Republicans, to endorse Nixon for Congress. He had also refused to indicate that a complimentary letter he had written to Voorhis, which Voorhis was using in his campaign literature, did not constitute endorsement of the Democratic candidate.) The scattering of Warrenites, however, muttered darkly that Nixon was giving the governor a "stab in the back."

The issues and the quarrels of the Republican convention are highly complex and not germane to this account. Nixon, however, figured prominently in one important battle. There were two delegations each from Texas and Georgia—one for Senator Taft, the other for Mr. Eisenhower. The Taft forces controlled the Credentials Committee and voted to seat their own delegations. The real test came on the floor of the convention, when the Eisenhower forces introduced the so-called fair-play rule. As a test of strength the vote on this issue was crucial—for if Taft won, he would have a substantial lead when the balloting on nominations began. And in this test of strength the California delegation was pivotal.

When the California delegation caucused on the "fair play" rule, a suggestion was made that it split fifty-fifty in its vote. Then Nixon entered the battle. He said that the rule—which would bar contested delegates from voting on contests involving other delegates—was either right or wrong. If the rule were right, and he argued eloquently that it was, then the

California delegates were bound to vote for it. The issue was clear—and so were the consequences of a yea vote. Senator William F. Knowland supported Nixon. The California delegation threw its weight in favor of the rule—and the stampede to General Eisenhower began.

On the morning of 11 July, the Republican National Convention nominated Dwight David Eisenhower as its candidate for the Presidency. Once that was done, Nixon, who had been up most of the previous night, decided that a little sleep would do him good. There had been some newspaper talk that he was being considered for the second spot on the ticket, and even an editorial in the Chicago *Daily News* which predicted that he would get it. But he had discounted the rumors, telling Pat Nixon that he wanted extra copies of the editorial "because this is probably the first and last time my name will be mentioned in connection with the Vice Presidency." He left the convention hall with Murray Chotiner and Bernard Brennan, friends and former campaign managers, lending his car to a reporter. At the Stockyards Inn where he thought he would be able to rest, he took off his clothes and tried to doze off.

But at the Blackstone Hotel, where Mr. Eisenhower had a suite, Eisenhower leaders were gathering to select a nominee for Vice President. Mr. Eisenhower was a little surprised that he was being consulted. As he said later, he had not known that he would have "any great influence" in the choice. While some twenty senators, governors, and national committeemen argued the merits of various candidates at the Conrad Hilton, the "inner circle" met with the President-to-be. Governor Dewey, Senator Henry Cabot Lodge, Herbert Brownell, Arthur Summerfield, and Senator Frank Carlson put the question to him. The phone rang. It was Senator Taft saying that he had a commitment to Senator Everett Dirksen and that he wanted to suggest his name. Dewey made a sour face; he had been the target of a violent attack by Dirksen the day before.

Mr. Eisenhower was reluctant to make any single suggestion. He had been out of the country for two years at NATO, he explained. Instead, he wrote seven names on a piece of paper. "Any one of these will be acceptable to me," he said. The name which led the list was Richard Nixon.* There was some general talk about Taft and Warren. But it was agreed that Taft would not accept the nomination and there was no enthusiasm for Warren. The group agreed that Nixon was the man—on the basis of his youth, his ability as a speaker and campaigner, the fact that he came from the key state of California, the national reputation he had gained as an anti-Communist, his outstanding record on domestic issues, and because it was felt that he would have the support of both the Taft and Eisenhower wings of the party.

Nixon's name was submitted by Brownell for the formal approval of the larger *ad hoc* committee at the Hilton. When the phone rang in Nixon's room, he reached for the receiver drowsily. A girl told him that Brownell wanted to speak to him. There was a brief lull—and Nixon could hear Brownell talking on another phone. "Hello, General," he was saying, "I wanted to tell you that the committee met and unanimously agreed on Nixon." Then he repeated the news to Nixon. "Can you get over there right away, Dick?" he said. "The general would like to see you." Nixon got dressed in a hurry. He needed a shave, but there was no time for that. Borrowing a car from the convention motor pool, he rushed to the Blackstone—a motorcycle escort's sirens screaming—where he was warmly greeted by Mr. Eisenhower. After introducing Nixon to Mrs. Mamie Eisenhower, the general told Nixon that he wanted to make a "crusade" of the campaign, with an emphasis on youth. "Will you join me in such a campaign?" he asked. "I'd be proud and happy to," said the still slightly dazed Nixon.

Pat Nixon received the news as she sat eating a sandwich

* The other six: (2) Lodge, (3) Governor Dan Thornton of Colorado, (4) Governor Arthur Langlie of Washington, (5) Governor Alfred Driscoll of New Jersey, (6) Knowland, and (7) Harold Stassen.

in a restaurant. "In the restaurant," she recalls, "an old movie was being shown on television. But just as I took a bite the movie was interrupted for a news bulletin that General Eisenhower wanted Dick as his running mate. That bite of sandwich popped right out of my mouth." She returned to the hall at a run.

At 5:25 P.M. Nixon appeared at the convention. His clothes were rumpled, he needed a shave, but the excitement had washed the weariness right out of his eyes. When the crowd spotted him, it stood up and cheered. Delegates pushed down the aisles to surround him and offer their congratulations. Wrote one reporter: "Nixon, tall and husky, looking more like a college crew man than like a senator, smiled and waved happily." The rest was ritual.

Senator Knowland, who had brushed aside earlier suggestions that he seek the Vice Presidential spot, made the nominating speech. Governor Alfred E. Driscoll of New Jersey was the first to second. In Nixon, he said, the Republicans would have a man as well aware of "the internal dangers to this country as General Eisenhower is aware of the dangers from abroad." Governor Frank A. Barrett of Wyoming boomed out, "No one has done more to put the fear of God into those who would betray their country." Governor John S. Fine of Pennsylvania moved to discard the roll call and to nominate Nixon by acclamation and the convention roared its approval. The delegates almost catapulted their new candidate to the platform. He stood there, raising his hands to the cheers of the delegates, smiling and laughing. Pat Nixon stood at his side during the demonstration.

This was the greatest moment in his life up to that time— and perhaps the greatest ever, no matter what new honors may come to him. For it was triumph unheard of and unexpected, and it came before he had been wounded and scarred by a campaign of vilification and falsification such as the country had not seen since the more primitive days of the Republic. Standing before the wildly demonstrating delegates, receiving the equally warm and spontaneous acclaim of all factions of a party which hours before had seemed irrevocably split, and deeply conscious that it is seldom given to a Vice Presidential candidate to stir up such an outburst of enthusiasm, he said to himself, "Here with the grace of God go I." It was a thought which returned to him when General Eisenhower made it known that, granting a Republican victory, he intended to enlarge the duties and responsibilities of the Vice President.

When he made his acceptance speech, however, he was not thinking in terms of personal satisfaction. He spoke of the need for a Republican victory which would give his party control of Congress. He lauded Taft as "one of the great senators," and pointed out that the victory he called for would make Taft the majority leader and give him a place of power in the nation's councils.

The next day Nixon became known as the busiest man in Chicago. He held two long conferences with Mr. Eisenhower; had a long private talk with Senator Taft; met with Republican Congressional leaders and with the National Committee; went into a huddle with Arthur Summerfield, the new National Chairman, and with Governor Fine; and talked to reporters who besieged him everywhere he went. The meetings with Mr. Eisenhower were to discuss in general terms the part each was to play in the campaign—and it was agreed that Nixon would carry more of the burden than is usually assigned to a Vice Presidential candidate.

For reporters he sketched in what he thought would be the two big issues to place before the voters—the Truman record and "communism at home and abroad." "Any Democratic candidate can be defeated on those issues," he said. "Regardless of who the candidate is, he'll be Truman-named and Truman-controlled." As to the Republican platform, which he had helped to draft, he was not entirely satisfied. It lacked directness, he pointed out, and should have been "much shorter, with less adjectives, more direct and simpler to read." The party, he guessed, would have to spell out its position on civil rights and labor legislation more explicitly. A reporter asked him what he felt about General Eisenhower's lack of political experience. Nixon grinned. "I've only been in politics a little longer myself," he said. "And there isn't much he needs to learn about politics that he doesn't already know."

The following day he was back in Washington with Pat and the two children. At the airport he was surrounded by reporters who asked him his plans. He was planning on taking his family to the beach for a short vacation, he said, but he intended to spend some of that time studying Mr. Eisenhower's views on the issues. "I'm, of course, generally familiar with the general's views," he said. "But before active campaigning begins, I want to familiarize myself thoroughly with everything the general has said. I must conduct my own campaign activities in complete harmony with the general. He has made great strides toward healing the wounds in the Republican Party. The fact that he went to call on Senator Taft instead of waiting for Taft to come and see him shows that he knows what to do to close the breach. I think that by November he will have a united party."

Two weeks later Nixon visited Mr. Eisenhower in the Colorado mountains. He was accompanied by five carloads of reporters. "Are you going to have a press conference?" the general asked. "I'm out of touch. I'll go inside and do the cooking." But he managed to put his running mate on KP, peeling potatoes, while photographers snapped pictures. Then Nixon pulled on some fishing boots and tried his hand at trout fishing. The temptation was too great for Mr. Eisenhower. He deserted the kitchen to give Nixon some expert instruction on fly casting. Nixon didn't catch any fish.

After dinner General Eisenhower and Nixon got down to business. It was at this meeting that the two men worked out the one-two campaign technique which proved to be so effective. It was agreed that, wherever possible, Mr. Eisenhower would stress the moral and positive campaign issues and appeal to the voters' "militant faith and hope" in his crusade. Nixon, on the other hand, would pound away at the flaws and weaknesses of the Democrats and of their candidate, Governor Adlai Stevenson, the reluctant dragon of Illinois. When the two men emerged to talk to reporters, Nixon told them that he and the general felt that "this shall be just as intensive a campaign as we can make it. We expect to conduct a fighting campaign on issues and facts and to bring our case to the people."

The polls gave General Eisenhower a commanding lead. But Nixon did not believe in letting pollsters decide elections. In 1946 all the polls had given Voorhis the election; in 1950, when Nixon's vote was overwhelming, the pollsters had predicted a week before election day that Mrs. Douglas had "the edge." Before the 1952 campaign got under way, he stated his views on the battle ahead. "I don't intend to take anything for granted," he said. "We're going to win—but only if we fight to win. It will be my job to cover as much of the country as possible, to tell the voters what's been going on in Washington and in the Far East. I'll talk about corruption and about communism. I'll explain what the Republican Party stands for—and what Stevenson and the Democrats stand for. That's how elections are won—not by sitting around to see what Mr. Gallup has to say. The great weakness in polls is that they cannot take into account the effect of an intensive, hard-hitting campaign."

Several days later he was putting his words into practice. Adlai Stevenson, he said in his first campaign speech, "is a captive candidate and he would be a captive President. He is Jack Arvey's candidate [Arvey was boss of the Democratic Chicago machine], and—this is his greatest handicap—he is Harry Truman's candidate." As for Senator John J. Sparkman, the Democratic Vice Presidential candidate, he was "an able man and a good friend of mine. But he is known in the Senate and in the South as a Truman man. The fact that

Senator Sparkman is on the ticket bears out what I said. Mr. Truman will control the ticket." Nixon was stating a political fact of life, for a restive Stevenson was forced to defend the record of the President—and it did him no good.

Nixon was the first to draw blood as the campaign progressed. The nation was bitterly disturbed over the news from Korea and the reports by responsible military leaders that the State Department wouldn't let them wind up the war in all-out victory. Stevenson foolishly opened himself up to attack on the Korean question. The specific instance was reported in *Newsweek*. "Stevenson claims to have a plan for bringing the war to a successful conclusion," the newsweekly disclosed, "but he says that revealing it would give the Reds vital military information." Nixon seized the opportunity by drawing the proper conclusions from the *Newsweek* story. In a formal statement he said:

> Mr. Stevenson is putting out bait for voters and working a cruel hoax on the men fighting and dying in Korea, and their families and loved ones at home, if he continues to leave the impression in the public mind that he has some magic formula which could bring the Korean war to an end on an honorable basis . . . Mr. Stevenson should tell the American people whether or not these reports are true or false. If he has had such a plan, he should have disclosed it to the Joint Chiefs of Staff, and if he has not done so he should do so immediately. Certainly he cannot contend that the Joint Chiefs would give his plan to the Communists. If he does not have such a plan, he should honestly tell the American people . . .
>
> Unfortunately, there are those who have come to expect double talk, fence-riding, and phoney promises from candidates for public office. Consequently, there may be a tendency in some quarters to excuse Mr. Stevenson for trying to play both ends against the middle. . . . If Mr. Stevenson or anyone in the Truman Administration has a plan to end the war, it should be put into effect now. The time for ending the Korean war should not be selected on the basis of the effect it may have on an election.

It was a sanguinary thrust, and its effects mounted. For Stevenson neither conferred with the Joint Chiefs of Staff nor repudiated the report that he had a "plan." Instead, he and his strategists tried to look mysterious and complained that Nixon was being unfair to them. But Nixon remained on the attack, swinging across the country, into California, and then up to the Northwest—bombarding the Truman Administration with ammunition collected by committees of the Democratic-controlled Eighty-first and Eighty-second Congresses. The crowds he drew were not as great as those which turned out for the Presidential candidates—but they were outsize for a Vice Presidential nominee. And they listened with the kind of attention which a Nixon audience may not bring with it but always develops.

Then the Democrats retaliated. The New York *Post* fired the first salvo in screamer heads about SECRET NIXON FUND. They could not know, in the flush of excitement, that the ricochet would strike Stevenson.

It is axiomatic that no man fights the Communists who wishes to preserve his reputation. For the Communists work ceaselessly and inexorably against those who have exposed them. They manufacture a mythology which by a kind of political capillarity moves upward and infects the thinking of men many stages removed from the Red phalanx. The Communists bide their time—and when it comes they let the venom rise. In the Senate of the United States, for example, there is a liberal solon who has on more than one occasion been carried from the floor drunk. By a tacit gentleman's agreement the Capitol press corps has never reported this. But should this senator ever join the "Red-baiters," several correspondents will undoubtedly discover that it is their "duty" to inform the American people of the situation. And so well and inconspicuously have the Communists worked, that they will have a non-Communist machine in gear to spread the news and make the senator's drinking habits a national issue.

In the case of Richard Nixon, the Communist apparatus had searched long and diligently to find something which could be magnified into scandal. They had tried on for size the "anti-Semitic" and "Jim Crow" tactic—and a few rash Democrats had picked it up. But in the face of the Anti-Defamation League's defense of him on this score, the attempt died a-borning. "The record of Senator Nixon is clear on the question of the hatemongers," said the ADL in its official publication, "there is nothing in that record which in any way would indicate that he had anti-Semitic tendencies or had participated in anti-minority activities."

There had been attempts to picture him as a ranting inquisitor and a foe of civil liberties. But the New York *Times*, which often differed strongly with Nixon, had written editorially of him on the day after he was nominated: "He has shown interest in the problem of protecting the rights of witnesses before Congressional committees. He has proved himself quite unafraid of leaving the party reservation when he felt the occasion demanded . . . [General Eisenhower] chose Senator Nixon—without benefit of 'deals'—for the Vice Presidency, on what we hope and expect will be a winning ticket in November."

There had been attacks during the Hiss Case—the standard charges that by "Red-baiting" Nixon was seeking publicity, and feathering his political nest by pushing the prosecution of Hiss to its logical conclusion. But the exigencies of the election campaign had silenced the newspapers which gave currency to this line. As the New York *Journal-American* pointed out, with justifiable amusement: "It causes us a certain sardonic satisfaction to remember that the publications which took part in that [campaign of sustained virulence] . . . have given their support to General Eisenhower . . . Now either they will have to accept Nixon, and in so doing admit that they were harmfully wrong about him, or they will have to support Eisenhower but oppose Nixon, which is a hell of a situation for a publication to be in."

On 18 September 1952, as the election campaign was warming up, the New York *Post*—a tabloid which commutes between sensationalism and anti-anti-Communism—"settled" the dilemma for those who were pro-Eisenhower but anti-Nixon. It devoted its entire front page to a block-type head: SECRET NIXON FUND. In a story which it modestly but inaccurately tagged as "exclusive," the *Post* charged that a "millionaire's club" had collected an 18,000-dollar "slush fund for Nixon's financial comfort." The story, by Leo Katcher, a screen writer who doubled as the paper's Hollywood correspondent, was, as *Look* magazine later said, the beginning of "a smear campaign without parallel."

This is the genesis of the story.

While in California Peter Edson, a columnist for the Newspaper Enterprise Alliance feature service, picked up a rumor, started by certain disgruntled Californians, that some of Senator Nixon's political expenses were being taken care of by a special fund. On 14 September, Edson interviewed Nixon on Meet the Press. After the telecast he asked, "Dick, what about this fund we hear about?" Nixon was neither surprised nor upset by the question. He had never made any "secret" of the fund and had, in fact, referred to it quite openly. He told Edson that if he wanted the details, he should get in touch with Dana C. Smith of Los Angeles—an old friend and the trustee of the fund. Edson called Smith by long-distance phone, got the facts, and wrote a straightaway news account which was in the mails to newspapers twenty-four hours before the *Post* got wind of it.*

The *Post* assigned Katcher to dig up the story, or a reasonable facsimile of same, which Katcher proceeded to do—working with Ernest Brashear of the Los Angeles *Daily News*, a strongly pro-Stevenson newspaper. Katcher's fanciful account appeared in the *Post* the same day as Edson's did in the Los Angeles *Daily News*. (Robert Smith, the general manager of the *News*, refused to publish Brashear's story. "I did some checking up on my own," he said, "and I was convinced Nixon had not used the money for personal living expenses. I'm not proud of the New York *Post* in this thing. I'm not running that kind of newspaper." *The New Republic*, somewhat more dedicated than Smith, eventually published the Brashear account.)

---

* Later, James A. Wechsler, editor of the *Post*, accused Edson in an editorial of stealing the story.

Nixon was campaigning in California when news of the
Post's "secret fund" attack reached him. He knew that the
operative word in it was "secret," although the fund had been
raised by Smith via a circular letter (dated 25 September
1951) sent to several hundred people and carefully describing
its purposes: for transportation to-and-from Washington so
that Nixon could keep in closer touch with his constituents,
payment of strictly political phone and telegraph charges,
preparation of political material and the distribution of
Nixon's speeches, radio and television charges, and the costs
of some 20,000 Christmas cards annually to Nixon campaign
volunteers and supporters. Nixon issued a statement acknowl-
edging the existence of the fund and adding that it had been
raised for "political expenses which I believed should not be
charged to the Federal government."

The consensus in newspaper and newsmagazine offices in
New York was that the *Post's* "fund" story was a dud. But
the editors had not counted on the industry of what is called
by liberals and Democrats the "one-party press." Newspapers
all over the country began to give the fund a tremendous play.
The Washington *Post* demanded that Nixon be dropped from
the ticket. Simultaneously reporters worked on Mr. Eisenhower's aides to get rid of Nixon. They argued that only in
this manner could the general assure his election. Honestly
perplexed by what was going on around him, Mr. Eisenhower
clearly showed his distress—and the pressures on him to force
Nixon's resignation increased. In the Northwest Nixon was
drawing huge crowds which applauded enthusiastically when
he defended his position, but this had no effect on Nixon's
detractors within the Eisenhower camp.

In the midst of the furor one Democratic voice spoke out
with restraint. "I am sure the great Republican Party will ascer-
tain [the] facts, will make them public, and act in accordance
with our best traditions," said Adlai Stevenson. Then, ignor-
ing the fact that the editor of the newspaper which initiated
the charges was a member of his "brain trust," Stevenson

magnanimously added: "Condemnation without all evidence, a practice all too familiar to us, would be wrong . . . I hope you will forgive me if I don't cut the enemy to ribbons. For the moment they seem to be taking care of themselves."

It was a full two days after the fund furor had begun that Nixon and General Eisenhower were able to communicate by telephone. "General, I'm only interested in seeing that you win," said Nixon. "If you think that my remaining on the ticket jeopardizes the chance to win, I'll turn in my resignation right now." Mr. Eisenhower, however, had not yet made up his mind. "Let's wait and see what all the facts are," he said. As James A. Farley was to point out later, an experienced politician would have decided then and there—one way or another. In this case inexperience dictated a course which, though tough and trying on Nixon, resulted in thoroughly turning the tables on the opposition. His "wait-and-see" stand took more courage than met the eye. Some of his more "liberal" advisers—particularly chairmen of Citizens for Eisenhower committees—were pressing him to fire Nixon without a hearing. (A tower of strength was Republican Chairman Arthur Summerfield, who stood by Nixon.) And the press corps on the Eisenhower train was muttering darkly of "whitewash" and making it known that in a private poll they had voted overwhelmingly against Nixon, which threw press secretary James Hagerty into a panic.

The pressure from these reporters was so great that Mr. Eisenhower was forced to call an off-the-record conference. "I don't care if you fellows are forty-to-two against me," he said, visibly annoyed at their extracurricular meddling, "but I'm taking my time on this. Nothing's decided, contrary to your idea that this is all a setup for a whitewash of Nixon. Nixon has got to be as clean as a hound's tooth." *

* The reporters who were accompanying Nixon stood by him loyally, though many were pro-Stevenson. After he took office, Nixon "created" the Order of the Hound's Tooth, issuing membership cards and an emblem to these reporters and to others who had displayed their continuing belief in his integrity.

The counterattack had already begun, however. Nixon issued a statement that he had "never received one penny of this fund for my personal use. This fund has been a matter of public knowledge from its inception; no attempt has ever been made to conceal its existence or purpose. All disbursements were made by Mr. Smith, by check, as trustee. Contributors to this fund are long-time supporters of mine who wish to enable me to continue my active battle against communism and corruption. None of them ever asked for or received any special consideration." In Los Angeles, Dana Smith gave the press copies of the letter which had been used to raise money for the fund. Contributions, it was noted, were limited to a range of 100 dollars to 500 dollars.

> The reason for the maximum [the letter said] was so that it can never be charged that anyone is contributing so much as to think he is entitled to special favors . . . I am writing you about it for a twofold purpose: 1st: So that when you see or hear of any money being spent on Dick's behalf you will know how it has been raised . . . 2nd: So that if you agree with the usefulness of such a program . . . and want to come in with us on it, you will know about it and have an opportunity to do so.

Dana Smith also gave the press a complete list of the contributors. It read like a *Who's Who* of southern California—men of sufficient sagacity who, had they need of a piece of a senator's integrity, would certainly have made the purchase in a less public manner. But none of this satisfied the "one-party press."

Three days after the story broke, a strategy meeting was called at the Hotel Statler in St. Louis. It was Sunday midnight when the meeting began. Present were Summerfield, Senator Mundt of the Republican speakers' bureau, Representative Leonard Hall, director of the Congressional campaign, and Robert Humphreys, the National Committee's publicity director. They discussed plans to put Nixon on a coast-to-coast radio hookup. Mundt suggested that television be included and Summerfield complained that the party just didn't have the money for this. It was generally agreed that the money would have to be spent, no matter what kind of a deficit it created.

"Get somebody out of bed in New York and arrange that show as soon as possible," Summerfield told Humphreys. There was one hitch. Humphreys called Murray Chotiner, Nixon's campaign manager, to tell him that a commercial sponsor would cancel his show and put Nixon on free of charge. But Nixon refused to go on a commercially sponsored program. At 2:00 A.M. Monday morning Humphreys called Chotiner to tell him that a nation-wide radio and TV hookup had been arranged, to be financed by the Republican Party, for that Tuesday night. General Eisenhower concurred. "Put the whole works on the record, Dick," he said.

At 5:30 P.M. that Tuesday, Nixon drove from his hotel in Los Angeles to Hollywood's El Capitan Theater, an NBC television studio. He had arrived in town that morning, relaxing briefly in the Ambassador Hotel's swimming pool and taking a long walk with William Rogers, now Deputy Attorney General. Then, after conferring with Chotiner, Rogers, Representative Patrick J. Hillings, and other advisers, he had made the final technical arrangements for the broadcast—vetoing the suggestion that a set representing his Senate office be built and insisting instead on a stock "library" set. He also turned down insistent demands that he rehearse his speech at the studio. The rest of the day Nixon spent alone, preparing his speech—filling legal-size sheets with the scribbled notes from which he finally spoke. Two hours before broadcast time he received the accounting of fund receipts and disbursements made by the firm of Price, Waterhouse, & Company.*

* The main items: Payments to airlines and hotels, as well as auto travel by Mr. and Mrs. Nixon, Murray Chotiner, and Bernard Brennan, $2,306.94; Joint Senate and House recording facility, $1,878.74; addressograph plates, $1,281.07; Christmas cards, $4,237.54; postage, $1,202.30; salaries for extra office help, $920.55; etc.

Nixon arrived at El Capitan some fifteen minutes before air-time. Technicians clustered about him, demanding some kind of rehearsal.* He refused flatly. "I don't want this to be or look like an act." His only suggestion was that Pat Nixon sit on the stage with him. "Will you get up or remain seated?" a querulous technician asked. "I don't know," Nixon replied. "Just keep the camera on me. I want to be completely free in my movements." Had he timed his speech? "I'm talking from notes," said Nixon, holding out five sheets of paper. "But don't worry about that." Just before the small red light on the camera flashed on, Nixon turned to his wife. "I don't think I can go through with it, Pat," he said. Then, facing an empty theater, he looked out at a radio and television audience of 55,000,000 people. He was on the air.

> My fellow Americans [he began] I come before you to-night as a candidate for the Vice Presidency and as a man whose honesty and integrity have been questioned. The usual thing to do when charges are made against you is either to ignore them or to deny them without giving details. I believe we've had enough of that in the United States . . . I have a theory, too, that the best and only answer to a smear or to an honest misunderstanding of the facts is to tell the truth. And that's why I'm here tonight. I want to tell you my side of the case.

And he told it—directly and without frills. There was emotion in his voice and his manner, for more than his political life was at stake. The "spontaneous" cry of "soap opera" from those hostile to him was a valiant attempt to make the American people forget what they had seen and heard that night. It was also an expression of a sick snobbishness. Two years later Cabell Phillips was to write an explanation of this for the New York *Times*.

* Some newspapers nevertheless have carried minutely detailed accounts stating how Nixon, in those fifteen minutes, rehearsed the speech, planned "effects," etc.

The gagster who first hung the label "All-American boy" on Nixon, probably did it out of malice. But there is a certain inevitability about the description. He is youthful, clean-cut, fresh, wholesome, and clear-eyed. There is a certain naïveté about him that is as misleading as it is charming . . . Cynics who make light of [his true personality] must reckon with the fact that it is an enormously attractive personality to millions of the uncynical, by whom they are heavily out-numbered.

One by one, in his speech, Nixon ticked off the points which showed that the accusations against him were false: It was no secret, every penny spent had been for purely political expenses, none of the contributors had received or even asked for any consideration in return. He reminded his audience that members of Congress made 15,000 dollars a year—and that virtually all of them had to supplement that income to serve their constituents properly. Some were rich, "but I don't happen to be a rich man." Some, like Senator Sparkman [his Democratic opposite number], put their wives on the government payroll. Some kept up their law business—a practice which often led to dangerous conflicts of interest when the client was doing business with the government.

He cited the accounting statement on the fund and read an opinion from a leading law firm that there was nothing illegal about it. "There's some that will say," Nixon went on, " 'maybe you were able to fake this thing. How can we believe what you say? After all, is there a possibility that maybe you got some sums in cash?' " To answer this question he detailed all of his personal finances: his 41,000-dollar home in Washington, with a 20,000-dollar mortgage; his 13,000-dollar home in Whittier (with a 10,000-dollar mortgage) where his parents lived; a loan of 4500 dollars from the Riggs National Bank in Washington; a debt of 3500 dollars to his parents; a 4000-dollar insurance policy, with a 500-dollar loan against it. "I own a 1950 Oldsmobile car. We have our furniture. We have no stocks and bonds of any kind." Pat Nixon had inherited 3000 dollars, he himself 1500 dollars. He earned an average of 1500 dollars a year from nonpolitical speaking engagements. He had received 1600 dollars over the past six years from estates which were in his law firm at the time he resigned.

"Pat doesn't have a mink coat," he said, poking at Democratic scandals, "but she does have a respectable Republican cloth coat." He made an ironic reference to Checkers, a dog his children had received as a gift. (This seemingly was the only part of the speech which registered with his opponents. They missed, or said they missed, the point entirely and attempted to depict it as sentimentality. They conveniently forgot a speech Franklin D. Roosevelt once made about a dog named Fala.)

"It isn't easy to come before a nation-wide audience and air your life as I have done. But I want to say some things before I conclude that I think you will agree on. Mr. Mitchell, the Chairman of the Democratic National Committee, made the statement that if a man couldn't afford to be in the United States Senate, he shouldn't run for the Senate . . . I don't agree with Mr. Mitchell when he says that only a rich man should serve his government . . . I don't believe that represents the thinking of the Democratic Party, and I know it doesn't represent the thinking of the Republican Party. I believe that it's fine that a man like Governor Stevenson who inherited a fortune from his father can run for President." But, he added, a man of modest means should certainly not be excluded.

After a discussion of the issues of the campaign Nixon said, "I don't believe that I ought to quit because I am not a quitter . . . But the decision, my friends, is not mine. I would do nothing that would harm the possibilities of Dwight Eisenhower to become President. And for that reason I am submitting to the Republican National Committee tonight through this television broadcast the decision which it is theirs to make. Let them decide whether my position on the ticket will help or hurt. And I am going to ask you to help them decide. Wire and write the [committee] whether you think I should stay on or get off. And whatever their decision is, I will abide by it."

When the little red eye of the camera blinked off, Nixon buried his head in his hands. "I couldn't do it," he said to Pat. "I wasn't any good." But the ordeal was not yet over. Before Nixon began his broadcast, Mr. Eisenhower had been meeting with a group of advisers in Cleveland. They agreed that if Nixon showed up well, he should be invited to confer with Mr. Eisenhower at his next scheduled stop in Wheeling, West Virginia. The Eisenhowers had watched the telecast in the manager's office at the Cleveland Public Auditorium, where the general was scheduled to speak that night, while a crowd of 17,000 heard it in the auditorium. When it was over, Mamie Eisenhower was weeping and the general's jaw was set to suppress his emotions.

"General, you'll have to throw your speech away," said James Hagerty, his press secretary. "Those people out there want to hear about Nixon." While Mr. Eisenhower scrawled notes for a new speech, the auditorium crowd was chanting "We want Nixon, we want Nixon." Representative George Bender, who was presiding, asked, "Are you in favor of Nixon?" and the crowd went wild. Thirty minutes later Mr. Eisenhower faced the crowd. "I have been a warrior and I like courage," he said. "I have seen many brave men in tough situations. I have never seen any come through in better fashion than Senator Nixon did tonight." Then he announced that he needed more than a single presentation and that he was asking Nixon to meet him.

The public response to Nixon's request broke all records.*

* Over 2,000,000 letters and telegrams were received by the Republican National Committee—350 to 1 in Nixon's favor. Western Union officials said they had never seen so great a volume of telegrams as they did that night. Letters which the National Committee received contained small contributions, but enough of them to cover the entire cost of the broadcast—75,000 dollars.

The switchboard at El Capitan lit up "like a Christmas tree," cutting Nixon off from a call that Summerfield was trying to put through, to explain why General Eisenhower wanted him to fly to Wheeling. Nixon merely learned that he was wanted there, but not that Ike had expressed approval—and he got the news from a reporter who had seen it on the wire. By the time Summerfield got through to the studio, Nixon was at the airport, bound for a speaking date in Missoula, Montana. He got the message to go to Wheeling, but despaired at the prospect of having to submit further to unwarranted humiliation. "What more can I explain?" he asked—and took off for Missoula.

It wasn't until late that night that Summerfield was able to reach him, and to tell him that the general was satisfied but that some advisers had persuaded him to delay his announcement in this fashion. When the Nixon plane reached Wheeling, Nixon was prepared to receive a hand-signal from Chotiner directing him where to meet General Eisenhower. A raised arm meant that Nixon would go to the hall where the general was to speak, both arms meant a meeting at the hotel. "And if I raise both hands and both feet," said Chotiner, "that means we are flat on our back." But Mr. Eisenhower was at the airport. He ran up the ramp and into the cabin.

"General, you didn't have to do this," said Nixon.

"You're my boy," said the general.

The Eisenhower accolade settled it. And it became obvious that the whole "secret fund" episode had backfired on the Democrats by giving new life to the entire Republican campaign. The attempt had left a bad taste in the mouths of many Americans. It had also demonstrated the hollowness of Stevenson's magnanimous statement when the New York *Post* story had first appeared. Even before the Nixon telecast the Democrats had begun to suffer. For it became known that Stevenson had an 18,000-dollar secret fund of his own—money left over from his gubernatorial campaign which he had used, he later said, to augment the salaries of deserving state employees.

Stevenson tried to ignore this disclosure—and then up popped a second fund. This one was brought to light by William J. McKinney, former head of the Illinois Department of Purchases under Stevenson. In a statement to the New York *World Telegram & Sun* McKinney said that the second fund was 100,000 dollars "or more"—made up of contributions from individuals and companies doing 35,000,000 dollars' worth of business with the state.*

Stevenson mopped his brow and finally admitted fund number one, but said that there was nothing wrong with it and that it was no secret. Prodded by the Republicans, Stevenson finally listed the contributors and recipients. But the press had no interest in the second fund—and Stevenson changed the subject by making his income tax returns public and demanding that Nixon do likewise. Nixon refused, though after his inauguration he released them. (They appeared in *Look* magazine.) No eager reporter pressed Stevenson on his silence over the second fund. But when Nixon took his family to Florida after the election, a newspaperman asked him graciously, "Is this on the vacation fund?"

Nixon had, however, succeeded in weathering the storm. He had been vindicated in the eyes of most Americans. Mr. Eisenhower had given him a rough time, but once it was all over, Nixon remarked with some justice, "If Ike would do that to me, you can be sure there will be no coverups or whitewashes in his Administration." But he knew that this first big attack had opened the flood gates. "This is not the last of the smears," he had said in the "fund" speech. Within hours Americans for Democratic Action was attacking "the Republicans and their propaganda spokesman" for daring to mention Stevenson's "explained" and unexplained funds, repeating the old canard that Nixon had voted solely with the

* It was claimed unofficially that this money was used to pay Stevenson's traveling expenses for speeches outside of Illinois and to help him with charitable contributions which he felt he had to make because of his political position. Stevenson himself has never denied the existence of the second fund—or explained its purpose.

"big interests"—and insisting that Nixon was therefore guilty even after he proved himself innocent.

The St. Louis *Post-Dispatch* made a frantic effort to prove that a refugee for whom Nixon had introduced a private bill to prevent deportation was really a Red. When this caused no flutter, twenty-three Columbia professors issued a "nonpartisan" statement, branding the Nixon fund "vicious" but arguing that the Stevenson funds were perfectly legitimate and honorable. Several of the professors (like Mark Van Doren and Richard B. Morris) were members of the pro-Hiss faction at Columbia; three had signed a statement urging the United States to drop all its atom bombs in the ocean; and nineteen were signers of a paid advertisement, "We are for Stevenson because . . ." which appeared in the New York *Times*.

On 30 October the St. Louis *Post-Dispatch* returned to the wars with a story that in April, 1952, Nixon had spent a vacation in Miami with the fund trustee, Dana Smith, and then had gone on with him to Havana—still as a guest—where Smith lost 4200 dollars at a gambling casino. The point of the story was obscure but it implied an improper relationship between Nixon and those who contributed to the fund. This attempt also died quickly. Nixon said flatly that it was a lie. A naïve reporter, who took the trouble to check the accusations against the facts, discovered that the *Post-Dispatch* was wrong. Between mid-March and 1 May Nixon's movements could be completely accounted for: he was not in Florida or Cuba, he had spent part of the time in a speech-making tour of Hawaii, and the rest where there was full corroboration of his whereabouts. (Two days before the election Drew Pearson repeated the fabrication.)

Pearson, who had attacked Nixon unremittingly since the Hiss Case, also broadcast to the country that Mr. and Mrs. Richard Nixon had signed a pauper's oath in California in 1951, several months before they made a 20,000-dollar down payment on their Washington home. "If Nixon lacked [the money] in March of 1951," Pearson asked, "where did he get [it] in July? This is a question the public has a right to ask of any candidate for office." Nixon demanded an immediate retraction, which he got—two weeks after the election, buried at the end of a Pearson column.

The most reprehensible attack of all concerned a "second fund" which Nixon was supposed to have. Democratic spokesmen made the charge and gilded it with a flat statement that Nixon and his family owned real estate "conservatively valued at a quarter of a million dollars." (How they arrived at that figure is a mystery.) In San Francisco to campaign for Stevenson, President Truman told a group of Democratic leaders: "Documentary evidence has been dug up linking Nixon with another fund. He won't get off the hook this time." Nothing concrete was published or said, but the whispers were that Nixon was the recipient of 52,000 dollars from oil interests.

The basis for these rumors was a forged letter which had been offered by a not-very shrewd public relations man, Roy de Groot, to Drew Pearson and the New York *Post*. It was such a palpable fraud that neither Pearson nor Editor James Wechsler felt it would be safe to use. The letter, purportedly written by H. W. Sanders, vice-president of the Union Oil Company, to Franklyn Waltman, publicity director of Sun Oil, said:

> To be certain that there is no misunderstanding in our conversation, let me explain that when I said we would be paying Dick Nixon more than $52,000 in the course of this year, I did not mean that all of it would come from our side . . . The remainder comes from our business friends in the area and from other sections of the oil industry . . . Feel free to call on him for anything you need in Washington.
> He regards himself as serving our whole industry.

After the election Pearson decided to use the letter obliquely by saying that if a letter in the possession of Sun Oil were published, it would destroy Dick Nixon. The letter was produced, and the FBI and a Democratic-controlled Senate committee moved in. Exhaustive hearings conducted by Senator Thomas

Hennings showed that Sanders had not written the letter—
and Waltman had not received it. FBI handwriting analysts
demonstrated that the signature was forged. Roy de Groot
testified that he had not offered the letter to either Pearson or
Wechsler until it had been declared authentic by an aide to
Democratic Chairman Mitchell. The Groot statement was
violently denied. There was talk of prosecution, but the election was over and no newspaper was sufficiently outraged to
make an editorial crusade of it.

Throughout the campaign there were other minor fabrications—all put forth with virtuous mien by the Democrats, even
as they complained that they were being smeared. Nixon paid
little heed. His campaign tour had become a triumphal pro-
cession, with crowds almost as large as those that turned out
for Stevenson and General Eisenhower. To the chagrin of the
opposition, his utterances were now widely reported. He was
not the forgotten man of political tradition, but a personality
in his own right.

On Boston Common, 10,000 persons in the Democratic
stronghold cheered him as he pleaded that they vote for Eisenhower "not as Republicans, not as independents, not as Democrats, but as Americans." In the state's industrial areas where
Nixon had pulled out a scattering of voters before his TV
appearance, he was drawing between 1500 and 2000 at
whistle stops. Downtown Boston was lined up two and three
deep along the sidewalks to wave to him.

The test of his drawing power came in South Boston—
"Little Southie"—a section so overwhelmingly Irish and Democratic that GOP campaigners have always passed it by completely. The Nixon motorcade pulled up in Perkins Square
and was immediately engulfed in a quiet but hostile crowd
of over 1000. Within minutes after Nixon began speaking,
the atmosphere had changed. By the time he finished, half
an hour later, the crowd was applauding its approval of his
attack on Communism and on the State Department, as well
as his praise of General Eisenhower.

Nixon, who spoke either off-the-cuff or from a few notes (even when he was being televised at Canton, Ohio, and Pittsburgh), made a direct nonpartisan appeal in his speeches. "America needs leadership," he said repeatedly, and of the two candidates, Eisenhower alone could supply it. The time had come to put "loyalty to country above loyalty to party." There was one issue, he insisted throughout the political swing, and that was national survival—both military and economic.

As the Truman-Stevenson attacks on Eisenhower increased in intensity, Nixon began striking back. The American people would "deeply resent the fact that their Commander-in-Chief is AWOL . . . when the United States is facing serious problems with Russia." The people did not love a "dirty fighter"; the attack would boomerang. He countered Adlai Stevenson's quip that Eisenhower was a "fancy khaki-colored package being sold by the political hucksters" by remarking at Allentown and Bethlehem: "If we're going to have color in this campaign, I'd rather have good old U. S. Army khaki than State Department pink . . ."

The Dick Nixon who faced the large turnouts was a somewhat different man from the Senator Nixon who had spoken to two or three hundred at a time before the "special fund" incident. He spoke longer to the crowds; five minute whistle-stops stretched into fifteen and twenty-minute speeches. The quality of earnestness and sincerity which had made him such a good vote getter in California seemed intensified—and the boyishness in manner and gesture were gone. He was friendly to the press, but he emerged less and less from the private car at the end of the fourteen-car special train. Working on a murderous schedule, shifting from train to plane and back to train, making as many as a dozen speeches a day, he was still tanned and vigorous. But the lines of fatigue were beginning to etch themselves on his face.

In mid-October he returned to nationwide television to discuss the Hiss Case, red herrings, and Adlai Stevenson. He accused the Democratic candidate of having disqualified himself for the Presidency by giving Alger Hiss a favorable character deposition for the first perjury trial in 1949. He also criticized Stevenson for attempting to give the impression that he had been ordered by the court to give the deposition, whereas it had been a voluntary act.

> Let me emphasize that there is no question in my mind as to the loyalty of Mr. Stevenson. But the question is one as to his judgment, and it is a very grave question. He has failed to recognize the threat [of communism] as many have failed to recognize it around him . . . Mr. Stevenson said, on September 13, 1952, "there aren't many American Communists, far fewer than in the days of the great depression. And they aren't on the whole very important." Compare that with the statement of J. Edgar Hoover [that the party is a well-knit, destructive force of 55,000, powerful far beyond its numbers].
>
> In his statement to the VFW, Mr. Stevenson referred to the Communists in the United States as being phantoms among us. In a statement to the Liberal Party he ridiculed those of us who were investigating the Communist conspiracy . . . as looking for them in the Bureau of Wildlife and Fisheries.

Nixon was being moderate. For at the time he had in his possession affidavits attesting to the fact that Stevenson's characterization in the deposition of his relations with Hiss as casual had been inaccurate. According to these affidavits, never denied by Stevenson though they were given currency in some papers, he had sought out Hiss for a speaking engagement in Chicago late in 1946 and flown out there to introduce him. Stevenson, however, was not impressed by Nixon's moderation. He answered in an *ad hominem* speech in which he rather plaintively accused Nixon of "sowing the seeds of doubt." Then he lashed out at John Foster Dulles and General Eisenhower—the former for bringing Hiss into the Carnegie Endowment for Peace, the latter for being a member of the board which voted, in his absence, to give Hiss a leave of absence during the trials.*

The campaign wound up with a big radio-TV rally in Boston at which General Eisenhower and Nixon spoke. Victory was in the air that election eve, and Nixon seemed to be carried away by its spirit. But privately he maintained his usual qualified pessimism. On 4 November, the voters went to the polls and gave the Eisenhower-Nixon ticket a landslide: 33,938,285 votes, 442 electoral votes, thirty-nine states. The campaign was over.† In six years Richard Nixon had risen from Representative-elect to Vice President-elect. Summing up, *Time* magazine said:

> The people did what materialists and cynics say people never do: voted against what they believed to be their immediate economic interests . . . [The campaign] was fought and won on transcendent issues of morality: (1) clean government, (2) government for all and not for special groups, and (3) government that would express in foreign and domestic policy the moral beliefs that lie at the root of U. S. life and greatness. Under the last heading comes the question of softness to communism, of which the confused deadlock of the Korean war was the most persuasive symptom and the Alger Hiss case the most clinically revealing symptom. Issues of this kind touched Americans of all classes—and the vote . . . reflected the judgment of all classes.

---

* This was an audacious move on Stevenson's part. Unless he was suffering from a lapse of memory, he knew that documentary proof existed which, if produced, would have made the appointment of Hiss to the Carnegie Endowment more embarrassing to him than to Dulles.

† There was one last flurry. When Dana Smith reported to the clerk of the House that $25,056.63 had poured in after the "fund" broadcast—and that it had been distributed to various Republican campaign groups which he itemized—the New York *Post* added that sum to the original $18,235 and charged "exclusively" that "there was a 'Nixon fund' of $43,291.63." It was a good try, but only the *Post* took it seriously. For those obsessed with Nixon's finances, it can be added that he resigned his Senate seat as of 1 January 1953 to give his successor seniority, thereby forfeiting by two days a 250-dollar-a-month pension.

He sits around in the parks, and feeds the pigeons, and takes walks, and goes to the movies. The other day he was going to join the library, but he had to have two references, so he couldn't get in.

So said Alexander Throttlebottom of himself in *Of Thee I Sing*—and the nation roared with laughter. John Adams, the first Vice President, found that his was "the most insignificant office that ever the invention of man contrived or his imagination conceived." With characteristic pungency Harry S. Truman put it more bluntly. "Look at all the Vice Presidents in history," he said. "They were about as useful as a cow's fifth teat."

President Theodore Roosevelt, who thought of his days under McKinley as "taking the veil," was the first man to do something about it. Enormously irritated by the perpetual tinkling of the tremendous "Jefferson chandelier" in the Executive office, he turned to an aide and said, "Get that thing out of here. I can't stand it any longer." It was a beautiful chandelier, purchased in France by Jefferson when he was Ambassador, and could not be scrapped. "What shall we do with it, Mr. President?" the aide asked. "Put it in the office of the Vice President," said Roosevelt. "He doesn't have anything to do. It will keep him awake."

But wakefulness only emphasized the fact that the Vice President had little to do beyond his Constitutional duty of presiding over the Senate. President Harding thought that it might be nice to have Vice President Coolidge sit in on Cabinet meetings. It added little to the festivities, but it filled a few of Coolidge's hours. President Franklin D. Roosevelt made Henry Wallace chairman of the Board of Economic Warfare. But Wallace, a veritable Mrs. Roosevelt of a Vice President, only got the Administration in trouble. When he was fired from the BEW, time lay heavy on his hands—and he used it to build himself up for the 1944 convention letdown.

Dwight D. Eisenhower knew what the Vice Presidency had meant when he asked Richard Nixon to become his running mate. Mr. Eisenhower was aware also that man is mortal. He had seen what happened when F.D.R. died and a Harry Truman, so unprepared that he did not even know of the existence of the atom bomb, was called on to assume the nation's highest office. In that meeting at the Blackstone Hotel, therefore, he told Nixon, "I don't want a Vice President who will be a figurehead. I want a man who will be a member of the team. And I want him to be able to step into the Presidency smoothly in case anything happens to me."

But other Presidents had said the same thing. And then, in the great isolation of their office, they had forgotten—or had been helped to forget by the aides and assistants who guard their own prerogatives with a fierce jealousy. Close friends, who watched Nixon standing quietly on the side lines as the giant light of the Inauguration festivities played on President Eisenhower, wondered whether he had been wise to leave the forum of the Senate. They had a feeling that a great career was being buried in what Jefferson had called the "tranquil and unoffending" role of the Vice President. They were wrong, of course, for President Eisenhower kept his word.

At the very start of his Administration he broke with all tradition by announcing that in his absences from Washington Nixon would preside over the National Security Council—a privilege assumed previously by the Secretary of State. Mr. Eisenhower also directed that the Cabinet would continue to meet when he was not in Washington—with Nixon in charge. The President's decision was of vast importance to Nixon. For the National Security Council is, in effect, the real government of the United States—outranking the Cabinet. It deals with the most sensitive areas of domestic and foreign policy, creating and coordinating the plans governing all activity from the cold war to atomic energy. Its members are privy to secrets so guarded that outside of its membership and staff they are known to no one except Joseph Alsop.

The confidence that President Eisenhower had in his Vice President gave Nixon a unique position. As President of the Senate, he was the only member of Congress to be a continuous and full-scale participant in Executive policymaking and administration. As such, he could serve the White House in the Senate—and bring the problems of the Senate to the President. His status in the Eisenhower Administration was further enhanced by the nonpolitical background of the Cabinet members. Men of brilliance like Treasury Secretary George Humphrey could advise the President on fiscal policy. But policy is wedded to politics—and Nixon was the only man on the team who had been through the basic training of electoral battle and the advanced study of the Congressional committee room.

When, for example, extension of the unpopular excess-profits tax was being discussed by the Cabinet, Nixon asserted that it would get through Congress—and that its potency as a political issue was highly overrated. "The national security," he said, "is more important than the elimination of an unpopular tax. If we show the people that national security is our first consideration, the country will go along." Again, when it was proposed that the military budget be cut, a few Cabinet members demurred on the ground that Congress would not sanction it. Nixon had argued against the cut, but nevertheless maintained that the President's prestige as a military leader would quiet any opposition—as, for a time, it did.

In his first two years in office Nixon imposed a kind of oath of silence on himself. The better to perform his duties, he decided that the Vice President accomplishes most who is in the headlines least. Offers of speaking engagements came in at the rate of about 500 a month—but Nixon turned them all down,* limiting such appearances to those which were official. He held no press conferences and kept interviews at a basic minimum. At first the opposition was stunned. It had been ready to leap at him the first time he opened his mouth. They began to refer to him as "Ike's errand boy" and "mother's little helper." When this brought no reaction, their suspicions were aroused. Obviously, they reasoned, he was up to something.

The simple fact was that he was busier than ever before in his life. Attending National Security Council meetings and the regular Cabinet sessions took time and preparation. Before Council meetings he was briefed very thoroughly by the staff on the problems to be discussed. He participated actively in the discussions and therefore had to know his facts and have them well organized. "You learn very quickly that the way to get along well with the President is to speak only when you know what you are talking about, to listen intently to what others have to say, and to make the presentation of a point as brief as possible," Nixon says. "There is nothing the President likes less than a long, windy presentation of facts. He likes to get right to the point without any extraneous discussion."

There were the strictly social aspects of his job. President Eisenhower, by preference, attended a minimum of the functions which occupy official Washington, so that it fell to Nixon to take over these duties. In his House and Senate days he had shunned these occasions as much as it was humanly possible, believing that "the cocktail party is the world's greatest time-wasting device." But invitations assigned to him

* At honorariums ranging up to 5,000 dollars. Nixon has refused all pay for speeches since he became Vice President. It is interesting to note that as of 1956 Nixon's net worth is 30,000 dollars—most of it his equity in his home.

by the President or the State Department had to be kept—and he learned to shave in his office and change into dinner or formal clothes in ten minutes by the stop-watch. He ruefully noted that once he was forced to make the change for eighteen consecutive nights.

A substantial amount of time was being consumed by office routine. An eager reporter, keeping a tally of the incoming calls, discovered that Nixon's telephone rang on the average of every four minutes. (When things are popping, it will ring every thirty seconds.) There was mail to be answered, impossible requests to be turned aside gracefully, conferences with legislative leaders, meetings, delegations to be received, important people to be seen who wanted to visit the President but settled for a handshake and a chat with the Vice President, newspapermen seeking information. There were visiting dignitaries to be met at the airport. On some days there were as many as twenty-five appointments to be kept.

As the Administration's representative in the Senate—and as the Senate's ambassador to the White House, moreover, he was faced with a touchy situation. The Senate of the Eighty-third Congress was divided equally between Republicans and the opposition. (Senator Wayne Morse had resigned from his party and become an "independent"—which gave the Democrats their forty-eighth vote.) He had to be on hand or close by to break any tie votes—he established a Senate record by breaking two in one day—and to persuade recalcitrant Republicans and reluctant Democrats to vote with the Administration. This required time spent in learning how individual senators felt about proposed legislation and Executive policy. Senator Lyndon Johnson, then Minority Leader, remarked on Nixon's efforts to be fair to the Democrats in his rulings and special appointments—and to keep them informed of what was going on at 1600 Pennsylvania Avenue. It was Nixon who learned that Senators Walter F. George and Richard Russell—both of whom swing tremendous influence among Democrats—were resentful that the President did not consult them on foreign policy. He suggested that Mr. Eisenhower invite them to lunch, which was done to the benefit of all parties concerned.

When legislation important to the Administration was up before the Senate, and passage was a touch-and-go matter, Nixon got to work. "I never ask a congressman or senator to vote a certain way," he has said. "I'd feel that was bad manners, an unpleasant experience for both of us. And it's very, very few times I'd get tough. I've got a temper—I expect I got it from my father—but the only time to lose your temper in politics is when it's deliberate. The greatest error you can make in politics is to get mad—and that's something I learned when I was a kid on the debating team. I believe in discussion. If there's something I want to get across to a man, I talk it over with him, we look at both sides of the question, maybe I indicate how the President feels about it, and then let nature take its course. Usually that works out fine."

To all this he added another time-consuming activity. It came to him partly by accident, partly because the Chowder and Marching Society which he had helped organize as a freshman in the Eightieth Congress was still a functioning institution. The instrumentality in the new activity was Representative Joe Holt of California, a onetime Marine who had arrived in Washington full of ideas, energy, and resolve. But after one quick and ineffectual briefing by the State Department, he was left stranded on the beach, with no tactical support from the Republican leadership in the House. As he tells it, he spent four months learning from the newspapers what was going on in the Administration. Then he went to see Nixon, who had helped him in the primary fight against Jack Tenney. And he explained that his situation was not unique, that other freshmen congressmen were as frustrated and isolated as he was. Would Nixon meet with this group and explain the facts of life to them?

Nixon agreed, telling them what the Administration was trying to do and discussing in great detail the vast complex of world problems facing the President. To his surprise he discovered that two thirds of the forty-five freshmen Republicans took an intransigent position against foreign aid of any kind—and frankly professed ignorance of many domestic problems. It was a two-hour session, during which he answered all questions and laid the Eisenhower policies on the line. "He sort of quieted our fears and made us realize that the Administration did have a program," Holt said later. This discussion of issues was so successful that the group began to meet regularly. Congressmen who could call themselves veterans began attending the sessions.

In Congress only the leadership is regularly briefed, and it tends to use the information it gets as a kind of prestige maker —dropping hints and feeding tidbits to the press. The average congressman, who feels remote from the center of power, welcomes any "inside information" he can get. Nixon supplied it, within the bounds of security and discretion. And he made use of the regular sessions to find out what was annoying the Congress, and what reactions it was getting from the voters. He told the President of these meetings, and Mr. Eisenhower was delighted. He had felt that the Republican Party did not do enough for its young people, and he hoped that through Nixon he would be able to groom some of the personable and talented junior congressmen for positions of leadership.

By midsummer 1953, Arthur Krock reported in the New York *Times* that "persons familiar with the Vice President's helpful activities have told this correspondent that they consider them unique in the records of his high office." Krock understated the case. Two members of the President's official family—according to some columnists the entire White House team hates Nixon—were willing to go far beyond Krock's evaluation.

> Most decisions in the government aren't made on the basis of philosophy, but on the basis of the dozens of events, personalities and situations that exist—in other words, the practical world calls for practical solutions [said one to *Life*

magazine]. In that context, Nixon is a man of principle—a man of principle who is also a great political tactician, and who works toward the ends he wants by means of political techniques.

Nixon is a vital part of our leadership [said the other member of the White House team]. For all practical purposes he's running the government here in Washington. He has impressed everyone. If you saw him at a Cabinet meeting, you would quickly recognize his stature vis-à-vis the other members of the Administration. He doesn't waste words. He gets right to the heart of the matter. He's realistic. From the political approach, he's very practical. But I think his judgment as well as his political acumen has impressed the Cabinet. More and more we look to him when we need help. There's no one more universally liked and he's always ready to pitch in and help . . . When a man produces, his reputation takes care of itself.

The highest praise of all came from President Eisenhower who said privately, "Dick is the most valuable member of my team." This expression of trust and affection was not lightly given. And with it went certain obligations. In September, 1953, the President called Nixon from Denver to ask him to attend the American Federation of Labor convention in St. Louis. Mr. Eisenhower told Nixon that it would be his assignment to read a Presidential message and then to speak informally to the delegates. Labor Secretary Martin Durkin had resigned from the Cabinet in a huff, accusing the President of lying, and the labor movement was spitting mad—at the President. Mr. Eisenhower wanted his record on labor spelled out, and he suggested also that Nixon make it plain that the Administration was not the captive of any segment of society but represented all the citizens.

It was a rough, tough assignment—and by ironic coincidence his appearance was scheduled for 23 September, the first anniversary of his "fund" speech. Nixon arrived in St. Louis and found no one from the AFL waiting to receive him.

As he entered the convention hall there was dead silence, broken only by a whispered message from delegate to delegate: "The word is 'chilly.'" The audience stared coldly at him as he began reading the President's message. There was no applause when he finished and began his own remarks. But Nixon ignored the chill and the derisive laughter which met his first words. He went straight to the point: Had the President lied to Martin Durkin? "There may have been a misunderstanding [laughter], but in forty years of service to his country, in the glare of publicity that men in public life must submit themselves to, Dwight Eisenhower has never been guilty of breaking his solemnly given word on anything, and I don't believe that anyone can claim he broke his word in this instance."

From there he went on to a defense of the Administration's labor policies. When he finished speaking, almost half of the audience rose and applauded, though many of them looked sheepishly and apprehensively over their shoulders as they did so. David Dubinsky, the president of the International Ladies Garment Workers and a shrewd politician in his own right, grinned. "That clever son of a bitch," he said. "He spoke right over our heads to the people." Reports reaching the White House on the effect of Nixon's speech showed that Dubinsky was right. The embarrassment engendered by the Durkin resignation was brought to a satisfactory conclusion. The next time the President saw Nixon, he grasped his shoulder and said, "I just want to thank you for that job out there." And to a friend, he remarked, "He's a good soldier. He stepped into a tough situation without flinching." *

The President chose the right word. For Nixon believed from the start that he should be precisely that—a "good soldier." In 1953 he told a reporter: "Controversies and conflicts

* The friendship which exists between the President and Nixon is reflected in the relations between Mamie Eisenhower and Pat Nixon. "You know, they say that the wives of Presidents and Vice Presidents never get along together," Mrs. Eisenhower said to Pat. "Let's show them that's not the case with us."

obviously make news. The Vice President, however, is supposed to support the President at all times and to echo the positions which the President may have taken." In all his public utterances, therefore, Nixon made it a strict point to reflect Administration policy—whatever his own views may have been. But in the privacy of the Cabinet and the National Security Council, when he differed with Administration policy Nixon expressed his own views with energy, occasionally convincing the others. There were other times, obviously, when he did not prevail. But once a policy had been established, he felt it was his duty, Constitutionally and out of personal loyalty to the President, to give it his full support.

He sided with Admiral Arthur Radford, the Chairman of the Joint Chiefs of Staff, on Far East policy. At National Security Council meetings he stressed the importance of maintaining strong defenses even at the expense of an unbalanced budget. He warned constantly of the Soviet threat when certain Cabinet members tended to minimize it. He was no advocate of "coexistence" which he realized from the start to be a maneuver aimed at lulling this nation into a series of diplomatic defeats. He energetically opposed the admission of Red China to the United Nations and gave strong support to Assistant Secretary of State Walter Robertson who shared his views. When forces within the State Department plotted to oust Robertson and to replace him with Arthur Dean—whose views on the Chinese Communist question were at best flabby —Nixon backstopped the Assistant Secretary quietly and effectively.

Sometimes he found himself in the middle of controversial issues. Senator John Bricker's amendment to restrict the President's treaty-making powers was introduced early in the first session of the Eighty-third Congress. This spelled trouble for the Administration, and the situation was aggravated by Chairman William "Wild Bill" Langer of the Senate Judiciary Committee. Langer, whose erratic motivations lead him to speak before an extreme right-wing group one day and to officiate at a Communist-front rally the next, wanted to hold hearings immediately. Secretary Dulles complained at a Cabinet meeting that he was not prepared to testify but that Langer had refused him a postponement. It fell to Nixon to arrange for a one-month delay. But he also reported to the President that the Bricker Amendment had strong support among many Republicans. Senator Lyndon Johnson, he said, had also told him privately that a substantial majority of Democrats (who remembered Yalta and Potsdam) supported some kind of restraint being placed on Executive agreements which committed the nation to far-reaching decisions. A bitter floor fight, Nixon suggested, would do the Administration no good—and it might destroy the Legislative-Executive cooperation which the President was seeking to foster. As a result the President ordered Attorney General Brownell to work out some compromise language on which Bricker and the Administration could agree. When no substitute wording could be found, the floor fight ensued, and the Administration was hurt despite the President's tactical victory.

As the first summer of Nixon's Vice Presidency drew to a close, he was given an assignment significant to the country and to himself. Shortly after Dulles had returned from a swing through the Near East, the President turned to Nixon at a meeting of the National Security Council and said, "Dick, I'd like you and Pat to take a trip to Asia after Congress adjourns." A good will trip, the President pointed out, would help dispel the false ideas about America prevalent in the Far East. The Asian nations had not been visited by anyone of the high rank of Vice President, and Mr. Eisenhower felt that a personal tour by Nixon would make American pledges of good will, respect, and interest more impressive.

Nixon accepted eagerly. And in his usual fashion he began to prepare for the trip—a 45,539-mile jaunt covering nineteen countries in ten weeks—by learning all he could about the areas he was to visit. The State Department supplied him with thick loose-leaf notebooks, one for each country, crammed with data on geography and people, government, economic and social conditions, United States Embassy officers, biographical data on the leaders, and a breakdown of the internal and external problems being faced. But he was determined that his trip would not be merely a round of official functions and private conferences with ambassadors and heads of state. He told State Department briefing officers that he wanted to mingle with the people wherever possible, to see and be seen. Though the diplomats expressed horror at the idea and attempted to dissuade him, this was precisely what he did.

Everywhere he went, he stopped his car, got out, and shook hands with people. Near Manila, a shopkeeper exclaimed, "He is not afraid to shake my hand even if my shirt is dirty." In Hong Kong a plainclothes man said, "He's quite a bloke, you know. He even talked to me." In Tokyo a small boy nudged a friend. "That's Nikushon," he said proudly. A correspondent wired: "The common touch may be old stuff to voters back home but it's new stuff to people of Asia. And judging by their reaction they like it. No American of Nixon's official stature has got out among the Asian people as much as he has." Another correspondent wrote, "The Nixons' Hong Kong accomplishment have cynical observers here shaking their heads in amazement."

Three years later he was to receive evidence of the continuing impact of his trip on at least one area he visited. "I thought you might like to know," the manager of an Afghanistani business firm wrote in December 1955, "some of the reaction which the Afghans have shown in connection with the present visit of Bulganin and Khrushchev . . . The Afghans are saying, 'Why is it necessary for Bulganin to bring all of these secret police along with him. When Mr. Nixon paid us a visit he did not bring any secret police with him. Mr. Nixon walked among the crowd of Afghans in Kabul and Kandahar shaking hands and never having any feeling that there was any danger.' It appears that your democratic way of shaking hands and greeting the man in the street is paying off."

The crowds which turned out to see this "democratic" American who smiled, shook hands, asked questions, plucked flowers from his wife's bouquet to give to children—and enjoyed doing it—were tremendous. There were also the ever-present Communist pickets and demonstrators, ready to make capital of any slip. In Burma thousands of people waited for him at a ruined pagoda in Pegu. A hundred or so Communists carried placards emblazoning the friendly message, "Go Back Warmonger, Valet of Wall Street," and a sound truck blasted out anti-American slogans. Nixon marched up to one of the Communists. "I notice these cards addressed to Mr. Nixon," he said. "I am Nixon, and I'm glad to know you. What's your name?" The Communist ducked into the crowd. To an English-speaking Red leader he said, "America doesn't want aggression. But what do you think of other aggressions such as Korea and Indochina?"

"That's different," said the Communist uncomfortably.

Nixon smiled. "Well, how many children have you got?"

Reported *Time*: "The closely-packed crowd roared with laughter; as Nixon pushed on, trying to shake hands with more demonstrators, they folded their signs and gave the whole thing up."

These were the outward manifestations. But he was also in contact with the leaders of free Asia, with native and colonial officials, with the best-informed Americans in the area. He talked with Chiang Kai-shek, with Syngman Rhee, with the French generals fighting a losing war in Indochina and the British generals holding their own in Malaya, with Prime Minister Nehru in India and Premier U Nu in Burma. He saw the Far East entire, as a boiling mass of contradictions, threats, and aspirations. In its rawest and most violent form he saw Communist aggression and subversion from the ringside seat of the Asian world. For the time being, he realized, the uncommitted peoples of Asia held the balance of power between the American-British complex and the Communist universal state.

When Nixon returned to Washington, he reported the observations and conclusions of his trip in a two-hour speech before the super-secret National Security Council. So cogent and penetrating was his presentation, according to an official who was present, that the President and the entire Council stood up and applauded when Nixon had finished speaking. The occasion, moreover, became a landmark in Nixon's career, for from that moment he became a respected participant in the nation's foreign policy councils. As he spoke, the Communists in Indochina had begun a great offensive against the French and Vietnamese—the offensive which eventually led to semi-collapse and the partition of the country.

Nixon warned that there was too much complacency among Americans over Indochina. If Indochina went, through a Red victory or a French deal, he reasoned, it would be followed by increased pressure on Laos, Cambodia, Malaya, Thailand, and most of southeast Asia. And if they were to go, then Japan would capitulate to the Communists, since a bulk of her trading was with that area. The problem was both military and psychological. "Every time they talk negotiation with the Reds in the French Parliament," he quoted a high defense ministry official in Indochina, "we lose 10 per cent of our Vietnamese effectives."

Nixon told the National Security Council that he had been quite impressed by President Syngman Rhee, whom he found shrewd and practical. Rhee, he felt, was the only man who could hold the Republic of Korea together, and the only leader who had the full support of the Korean people. (He quoted Sir Gerald Templar, commanding British troops in Malaya: "I don't like the man, but what Indochina needs is another Syngman Rhee.") He felt reasonably sure that Rhee would continue to cooperate with the United Nations forces in Korea—unless the Communists violated the truce by outright aggression. But with Red China incorporating North Korea into its territory, Nixon realized that Korean unification, which the State Department was vainly attempting to achieve by negotiation, was impossible.

Expressing deep concern over Africa, he said that the situation was touchy—particularly in the north and south. The Indian foreign service was conniving against the West in that region, as it had been doing throughout Asia. The Communists, moreover, had their sights on Africa and had begun to concentrate their forces. As the world's resources move toward depletion, he said, Africa would become decisive. And, he pointed out, the Communists had a sense of history; they were planning twenty-five years ahead for Africa. The United States planned only from one crisis to the next, from one pact to the next. If America was to survive, it would have to begin thinking in long-range terms.

Nixon urged the creation of a military crescent—including Turkey, Iran, Pakistan, Indochina, Formosa, and Japan—to close the ring around the Sino-Soviet empire, and in this strategy he got strong support from Admiral Radford and the Joint Chiefs of Staff. He called for the implementation of this defensive arrangement by some sort of Asian equivalent to the North Atlantic Treaty Organization. He argued for military aid to Pakistan, which was then a subject of high-level debate and was eventually carried through, as a counterforce to the confirmed neutralism of Jawaharlal Nehru's India. Nixon had talked at length with Nehru, and he had returned from his trip convinced that India's neutralism was an outgrowth of the prime minister's belief that India could be a dominant force only if the rest of non-Communist Asia were weak and unarmed. Nehru was contemptuous of flattery and respectful of strength—hence Nixon's conclusion that American policy must be based on what was best for the United States, not on any fear of India's reaction.

On Nixon's return from Asia and Africa, he learned that the pro-Red China element had planted rumors which resulted in widespread press reports from the usually "reliable sources" that he favored recognition of Red China. He took the opportunity to restate his categorical opposition to such a step. Any attempts to bring Communist China into the family of nations, he insisted, should be blocked by all the means at America's disposal. For, he noted, Formosa was more than a military bastion. It was the rallying point for 13,000,000 overseas Chinese who were playing a significant part in the affairs of other Asian states. Recognition of Red China would, in effect, hand over these expatriate Chinese to the Communist world.

In the weeks that followed, Nixon also reported to television and other audiences. In his public presentations, however, he stressed factual material and steered clear of observations and conclusions which impinged on the foreign policy prerogatives of Secretary Dulles and the State Department. What he said was to a degree "controversial," for many Democrats and some Republicans took the line that the United States should recognize Red China and jettison the Chinese Nationalists, should oust President Rhee, should kowtow to India at all costs.

At the height of the controversy Nixon addressed the annual convention of the American Society of Newspaper Editors, taking as his subject, "the most important issue confronting the United States . . . the war for Asia." He asked that he not be quoted on matters which might fall to the prerogative of the President or the Secretary of State, or on conversations with chiefs of foreign states which protocol decrees may be made public only by the chiefs of state themselves. The speech was long and gave great detail to substantiate his opening characterization of the situation in Asia. Numerous editorials, such as the one in the New Orleans *Times-Picayune*, characterized it as "a brilliant exposition" and added, "But it was Mr. Nixon's personal qualities—his cogency, clear thinking and force—that most impressed the editors."

But a curious storm blew up over that speech, as a result of one question put and answered informally. Talbot Patrick, editor and publisher of the Rock Hill (South Carolina) *Evening Herald* asked, "The Government of France, if it should decide to withdraw French troops from Indochina, do you think that the United States should send in American troops to replace them if that were necessary to prevent Indochina being taken over by the Communists?"

Nixon replied carefully, ". . . I do not believe that the presumption or the assumption which has been made by the questioner will occur and I recognize that he has put it as a hypothetical question . . . however, answering the question directly and facing up to it, I say this: The United States is the leader of the free world and the free world cannot afford in Asia a further retreat to the Communists. I trust that we can do it without putting American boys in. I think that with the proper leadership we can do it without putting American boys in. But under the circumstances, if in order to avoid further Communist expansion in Asia and particularly in Indochina, if in order to avoid it we must take the risk now by putting American boys in, I believe that the Executive Branch of the Government has to take the politically unpopular position of facing up to it and doing it and I personally would support such a decision." (Applause.)

Within hours there appeared news stories of a "trial balloon," and not long after, Nixon was identified in the press as the balloonist. It became a part of the anti-Nixon mythology that he had proposed "another Korea" by means of a "planted question." And criticism of Nixon, which for a time had taken a more legitimate form, returned to its old *ad hominem* nature.

But 1954 was to be the year in which the McCarthy controversy came to its climax and overshadowed everything else. And it was an election year. Nixon was to play a part in each—in the one reluctantly, in the other willingly, with unforeseeable results in both.

13. NIXON, MCCARTHY, AND AN ELECTION

The Sulgrave Club in Washington is what feature writers like to call "swank." On the night of 12 December 1950, however, it was the setting for a one-act, two-scene playlet hardly in keeping with the club's elegance. The occasion was a small party at which Senator Joe McCarthy, Drew Pearson, Senator-elect Richard Nixon, and Representative Charles Bennett were among the guests.

SCENE ONE (*at dinner*)

McCarthy (to Pearson): I'm going to give a little talk about you on the Senate floor tomorrow. I'm going to say some things about you the country should know. I thought you'd be interested.

Pearson: I have some things to say about you. My column has greater circulation than the *Congressional Record*.

McCarthy: There's nothing new you can say about me. I've been called everything in the world.

Pearson: I haven't gone after a man yet that I haven't gotten in the end.

McCarthy: Well, Drew, I just wanted to tip you off.

Pearson: Why don't you give them a speech about your income tax? Tell them how you keep out of jail.

(*McCarthy stands up and seizes Pearson by the neck. Bennett, who is lame from a polio attack, tries to separate the two men and slips to the floor. While McCarthy helps Bennett up, Pearson exits left.*)

SCENE TWO (*later, in the cloakroom*)

McCarthy (*slapping Pearson heartily on the back*): It was a pleasant evening, wasn't it, Drew?
>   (*Pearson flushes, then shoves his hand into his pocket threateningly.*)

McCarthy: Don't you reach into your pocket like that!
>   (*He grabs Pearson's arms, moves forward. There is a brief struggle. Then McCarthy slaps Pearson twice, resoundingly. Nixon enters. He sees what is going on, and intervenes, separates the two men, and pulls McCarthy away.**)

Nixon: Let's go, Joe.

McCarthy: I won't turn my back on that son of a bitch. He's got to go first.
>   (*Pearson slips away.*)

CURTAIN

This was not the first time that Nixon had moved in behalf of McCarthy, nor was it to be the last. As a man whose anti-Communist reputation had been made in meticulously proper investigation, Nixon felt a certain responsibility for McCarthy or for any other individual who took up the fight against communism. He was experienced enough to know that the great subterranean forces of pro-Communist and anti-anti-Communist persuasion were ever-watchful, and that they visited the mistakes of one anti-Communist on all anti-Communists. During his tenure with the House Un-American Activities Committee he had been partially successful in imposing a code of behavior which protected the rights of witnesses without allowing them to make a Roman holiday of

---

* Later Nixon told friends, "I never saw a man slapped so hard. If I hadn't pulled McCarthy away, he might have killed Pearson." The following day twenty-four senators, many of whom had been smeared by Pearson, called to congratulate McCarthy. And Senator Arthur Watkins, who four years later was to preside over the censure of McCarthy's rough methods, stopped him at the Capitol to add his own words of praise and commendation over the encounter.

hearings.* In 1949, when the Democratic majority of the committee proposed a Congressional investigation of textbooks, he had opposed the investigation in a public statement, arguing that legislators were not competent to handle so technical and touchy a job—and that it would lay committees open to the charge of "book burning." "Unquestionably," he said, "an exhaustive inquiry by a qualified nonpolitical body is needed . . . The correct procedure would entail the establishment of a commission of educators composed of such men as General Dwight D. Eisenhower, president of Columbia University, and Dr. Henry M. Wriston, president of Brown University."

In all his acts as a Congressional investigator, he had been motivated by an inborn sense of fairness. But he was always fully aware that those who were bitterly opposed to the exposure of Communists had the shrewdness to attack not *what* was being investigated, but *how* the investigations were being carried out. During the Hiss Case he had robbed them of an issue by moving forward with impeccable circumspection—and the Hissites, conscious that they had been checkmated, took out their frustration by questioning the validity of the jury system. Nixon knew, moreover, that the attack on anti-Communists was usually directly proportionate to their success in arousing the country from its complacency. And there was no doubt that on this score McCarthy was doing very well.

Shortly after the 9 February 1950 speech which launched Senator McCarthy on his phenomenal career, Nixon met with him. It has been forgotten by everyone, including McCarthy,

* The Nixon code: "Each witness should be allowed to present a statement in his own behalf where charges have been made against him before the committee. A witness should be allowed to submit the names of prospective witnesses who will testify in his behalf where charges have been made against him. A witness should be allowed to submit questions which he feels should be asked of individuals who have made charges against him. Televising of committee hearings should be prohibited because it places an unreasonable burden on the average witness."

that the point of the Wheeling speech was not the exposure
of new and startling facts about Communist infiltration of
government, but a denunciation of the Truman Administration for steadfastly refusing to make use of documented information about Communists and chronic fellow travelers
in the Federal establishment. That the facts were known but
ignored was precisely the issue—and it was a damaging indict-
ment. It was an issue which Nixon and the Republican Party
had frequently stressed.

When he discussed the speech with McCarthy, Nixon knew
that the material in it came from files of several Congressional
committees. This was all to the good, for it strengthened the
point. But he recognized that the Democrats were trying to
shif the argument to another area: Was McCarthy's information "new" or was it "old stuff"? He warned McCarthy not
to destroy his case by being led down the garden path to
ground where the Democrats could obscure the primary issue. And he urged McCarthy not to overstate his case, to
allow the facts to speak for themselves without hyperbole.
"Apparently," Nixon says, "I did not make too much of an
impression on him in this respect, although in the times I have
seen him since then I have repeatedly counseled him to follow
this course."

McCarthy, however, was a rough-and-tumble fighter. His
personality, his whole attitude toward life and politics, differed from Nixon's. He approached all problems with a
combination of mercurial Irish and stolid German. Subtleties
and distinctions were not of his liking, and he could not see
why he should split hairs with people who for whatever reason were covering up a terrible condition. He listened to
Nixon because he could respect the motives and the knowledge which prompted the advice. But he could not curb his
impulses or throw away his shillelagh. When Nixon offered
him the use of his files to help document his charges, Mc-
Carthy gratefully accepted the offer—particularly in the

period during and after the brazenly partisan Tydings Committee "investigated" his charges.

In his Senate years Nixon was busy against the influence peddlers and the Truman cronies. And McCarthy was focusing his efforts on the State Department's pro-Chinese Communist cabal, and a conspiracy so pernicious that even his most unrestrained statements were usually an understatement of the facts. The tide was running with McCarthy, for the evidence was so incontrovertible that even Secretary Acheson was forced to pay it some heed—and even to fire a few of the "security risks" in his bailiwick. The troubles began for both Nixon and McCarthy after January, 1953, when a Republican President sat in the White House and the Republican Party controlled both House and Senate. McCarthy was —and is—basically a maverick. He did not accept party responsibility. And he felt, with some justice, that he had contributed much to the Republican victory. Nixon, on the other hand, was a spokesman for the Administration. He believed, moreover, that continued Republican victory depended on cooperation among the various elements in the party. The situation was further complicated by some of the President's friends—people like Paul Hoffman—who had dedicated themselves to the destruction of McCarthy and lost no opportunity to stir up ill feeling against him in the White House. They were doing their utmost to make the Democratic concept of McCarthy the basis of Republican policy toward him.

Nixon's view on McCarthy, which prevailed for a time, was that it would be morally wrong and politically suicidal to attack the Wisconsin senator when he was right. He advised members of the Eisenhower team to examine each individual act of McCarthy's and then to support him when he was right, to criticize him when he was wrong. This position, of course, brought him into conflict with those in Congress and the country at large who made it an article of faith that McCarthy was never wrong. It equally angered those whose own article was that McCarthy was always wrong. Nixon felt that it was his duty to act as a brake on the excesses of both camps. Talking to a reporter in the summer of 1953, he summed it up this way:

> I have never discussed with the President any of the specific actions I have taken with regard to McCarthy. I have generally proceeded in each instance on my own initiative. I feel that I know the President's views on the whole issue, and I think it is the responsibility of all of us who are working with him to bring just as few problems to his personal attention as is necessary. My theory as far as relations with McCarthy are concerned is that while the President would undoubtedly win in any head-on clash with McCarthy, he could not help but be hurt in the process. A controversy would cause a very decided split among Republicans and could well lead to defeat for us in the 1954 elections. There may be a time when as a matter of principle the President may have to become involved in such a fight. But I think it is the responsibility of all of us to avoid it as long as we possibly can. It will give aid and comfort to no one but the Democrats. It is interesting to note that many of the columnists who have been taking the President to task for not attacking McCarthy are neither friends of McCarthy nor of the President—before November, 1952, that is.*

With this in mind, Nixon interceded successfully on a number of occasions. When James Conant was nominated High Commissioner for Germany, the President asked for speedy action by the Senate. McCarthy had already indicated that he intended to make a public fight on the floor against Conant. "I talked to McCarthy," Nixon says, "and told him that I thought it would be unwise for him to do so for two reasons. One, because he was going to lose and therefore from his own standpoint would suffer a defeat early in the session, thereby hurting himself immeasurably. Two, it would be detrimental from the standpoint of the country for Conant

* It may be added that some of those urging McCarthy to take on Mr. Eisenhower were Democrats who have since turned up as strange bedfellows of the New Deal-Harriman wing of the party.

to go to Germany after being attacked on the Senate floor."
At Nixon's suggestion McCarthy wrote a letter to the President, expressing his opposition but promising not to make a
fight over it.

Again, when Ambassador to Russia Charles E. (Chip)
Bohlen's name was sent to the Senate, Nixon made it a point
to find out what was in the FBI file. When he learned that
there was no information derogatory to Bohlen, he tried
to get McCarthy to hold off on an attack. McCarthy refused,
but the ground was cut out from under him—and many pro-
McCarthy senators who would have opposed the appointment
voted in its favor. It is interesting to note that though some of
his followers muttered of a "sellout" by Nixon, McCarthy
himself toned down his attacks during the debate on Bohlen
and—in fact—privately conceded that Nixon had acted
properly.

Nixon was forced to act again when the McCarthy Committee took up the question of East-West trade, and the ship-
ment of strategic materials to Iron Curtain countries. There
were loopholes in the law, and McCarthy had repeatedly
clamored for some kind of Executive action. Finally he called
together a group of Greek shipowners who were doing business with Red China and got them to sign a "pact" that they
would cease and desist. With the exception of doctrinaire
liberals and business interests profiting from this trade, most
Americans applauded this achievement. Mutual Security Director Harold Stassen, however, took umbrage. He appeared
before the McCarthy Committee and, in an undignified display of pique, accused the chairman of "undermining" United
States foreign policy. Nixon brought Secretary Dulles and
McCarthy together to iron out the dispute. Dulles issued a
statement that the "pact" was "in the national interest" and
McCarthy agreed to keep the department informed on any
further "foreign policy" moves on his part.

The incident was not closed, however. Senator Stuart
Symington, a Democratic member of the McCarthy Commit-

tee, realized that the Red trade issue had political possibilities. He suggested that McCarthy write a letter to President Eisenhower asking for a formal statement of his position on Allied trade with the Reds. The Symington booby trap was well conceived. It put the President in the embarrassing position either of ducking the issue or of making a categorical statement which would cause trouble for him at home or abroad. When Nixon learned of the letter, he telephoned McCarthy and pointed out that the only beneficiaries would be Symington and the Democrats. McCarthy agreed and asked Nixon to withdraw the letter, in the hot hands of the White House staff at the time, before it reached Mr. Eisenhower.

On these issues Nixon was willing to act as the conciliator— or to back McCarthy. There were others on which he thought McCarthy was dead wrong—or compromising a proper position by sloppy action. It was Nixon's conviction that basically the Voice of America served a useful function. It had flaws, of course, and it needed to be cleansed of Truman holdovers. To investigate it was certainly the function of Congress. But he did not believe that McCarthy's hearings—dramatic but full of factual bobbles—or the venture into Europe of Roy Cohn and G. David Schine—a highly distorted and misrepresented "junket" but nevertheless a fiasco—was the way to go about it. Nixon felt that McCarthy had played into the hands of the opposition by subpoenaing New York *Post* Editor James Wechsler. He did not take seriously Wechsler's posture of martyrdom or any of the crocodile tears over a "threat" to "freedom of the press." But he reasoned that it was a foolish move—and one that compromised the integrity of Congressional investigations.

McCarthy, moreover, had begun to spread himself too thin. Investigations were begun and never brought to a conclusion. Conflicting testimony of witnesses was permitted to remain in the record unchecked. McCarthy was everywhere—speaking, attacking, defending, accusing. Whether or not his accusations proved to be true—months later—made little difference. The clean-up job was left for others. Nixon was appalled by the tremendous campaign of vilification against McCarthy—the preposterous charges and the unprintable rumors—but as McCarthy progressed toward a break with the Administration, particularly on the tactics of the Red trade issue, Nixon's sympathy turned into irritation.* It was difficult to defend a man who called for the defeat of members of his party, as McCarthy had done, because they refused to be committed on the Red trade question—no matter how important that issue might be. It was even more difficult when McCarthy began to hint that the Eisenhower Administration was "soft on communism."

Had Nixon been in control of the situation, he would have remained silent while the Democrats shouted themselves hoarse over the mythical monster they invoked in their attacks on McCarthy and "McCarthyism." Nixon was not deceived by the unceasing campaign that McCarthy must go—or by the Democratic pleas to the President that he must crush McCarthy for the good of the Republican Party. He knew, as did the Democrats, that the McCarthy issue had caused millions of traditionally Democratic voters to bolt their party in 1952. If McCarthy and the Administration could be forced to a showdown, these voters would either stay at home in the 1954 elections or return to their party—which was what the Democratic National Committee had in mind. The press campaign, however, had its effect on the President. In mid-March, Adlai Stevenson tried to pin the "McCarthyism" label on the Eisenhower Administration, and Nixon was selected to make the Administration's answer. In speaking on the subject of McCarthy, Nixon sought to dissociate himself and his party from the senator's catch phrase, "twenty years † of treason"

---

* Nixon, however, despite widespread reports to that effect, did not try to divert McCarthy from investigating communism in government. McCarthy himself was quoted by the Chief of the International News Service Washington Bureau, David Sentner, "Dick Nixon has never asked me to stop my investigations into communism."
† And in 1954, "twenty-one years of treason."

which allowed the Democrats to interpret it as charging that Democrats belonged to the "party of treason." And he wanted to put the whole controversy in its proper perspective. Without mentioning McCarthy, he said:

> Men who have in the past done effective work exposing communism in this country have, by reckless talk and questionable methods, made themselves the issue, rather than the cause they believe in so deeply. When they have done this, you see, they have not only diverted attention from the danger of communism, but they have diverted that attention to themselves . . . [But] we must remember that the extremes of those who ignored the Communist danger or who covered it up when it was exposed have led to the extremes of those who exaggerate it today.

Here was a commendation for McCarthy's past achievement in the Communist fight and a warning that he was no longer keeping his eye on the ball. McCarthy brushed the Nixon speech aside—it didn't refer to him, he said—and within hours had returned to the controversy which eventually led to the disastrous Army-McCarthy hearings.* Before 12 April 1954, when the thirty-six-day circus began, Nixon had been working energetically to forestall an airing of soiled linen such as the country had seldom seen. It was his contention that all the hearings could possibly achieve was destruction of Republicans and Republican defeat at the polls in Novem-

* The controversy was sparked by the Peress Case and the less-than-candid testimony of Brigadier General Ralph Zwicker. On this score McCarthy was in the right—though somewhat hyperbolically so. The collateral issue of Roy Cohn and David Schine's commission was an afterthought of the Army Department. It is this writer's belief that the Cohn-Schine matter was the pernicious factor, from McCarthy's point of view. Had Cohn resigned, the hearings would have stressed the Peress Case. With Cohn still on the scene—and making no move to resign—McCarthy was forced to defend what was basically indefensible. Out of loyalty to two staff members he did very serious damage to himself. It is significant that Senator John McClellan's inexorable pursuit of the Peress Case, in 1955, proved McCarthy's point that the Army Department had been remiss in its handling of security risks, and that the Army's rebuttal to McCarthy's charges had been far from frank.

ber—a fact which the less politically sophisticated members of the White House entourage were unable to grasp. In the debate Nixon argued that the agitation for the hearings was a shrewd Democratic maneuver. He predicted that neither side could win the test of strength between McCarthy and the Administration. When the hearings ended in mid-June, Nixon's point had been abundantly proved—but by that time it was too late.

(Many months later, Nixon summed up his views on McCarthy. "McCarthy and I broke when he attacked the Administration," he said. "I did my best to avoid this break not only because I thought it would be harmful to the party and to the Administration, but because I felt that it would be harmful to the cause of those of us who had been engaged for years in the anti-Communist fight. To me, the greatest disservice McCarthy has rendered is to that group of anti-Communists. McCarthy's intentions were right, but his tactics were, frankly, so inept at times that eventually he probably did our cause more harm than good.")

The end of the Army-McCarthy hearings left the Republican Party shattered, committed to a farcical "censuring" which served no purpose but to spin out a grotesque ritual for which not even the high priests showed any enthusiasm. Inevitably the Taft-*vs.*-Eisenhower antagonisms of the 1952 convention came to life again. Professional politicians blamed the "amateurs" for the party's troubles. At the grass roots Republican workers showed apathy. In contrast, the Democrats were exuberant. They had driven the Republicans into a bloody civil war. In the big urban centers of the East, where the Catholic vote is of crucial importance, Democrats had begun to regain lost ground. They listened with simple joy to Republican misgivings that a great Democratic sweep was in the making. Then, in September, the Maine elections brought a stunning upset when the traditionally Republican state elected a Democrat governor.

On 15 September, Richard Nixon set out from Washington in a chartered United Air Lines Convair on an election tour of fantastic proportions. It was fantastic not merely in scope but in the trust which the President and the Republican National Committee placed in him. He was their last, best hope of snatching moderate defeat from the jaws of utter collapse—and Republican leaders made no bones about it, though they still spoke of "victory" in November. Writing for the New York *Times*, Cabell Phillips said of Nixon's role: "He is not only the chief strategist of the campaign now being waged across the country, he is its main assault force."

In forty-eight days Nixon visited ninety-five cities in thirty-one states, flew nearly 26,000 miles, delivered 204 speeches, and held more than a hundred press, radio, and television conferences. He dictated a minimum of three press releases a day to his secretary, Rose Mary Woods, and substantial excerpts of forthcoming speeches to newspapermen who had to write their stories in advance of the actual addresses. In the last three weeks he slept a maximum of four hours a night. "In the amount of effort expended, the distance covered, the words spoken and written, the hands that were shaken, the indigestible banquet lunches and dinners swallowed down," said Washington correspondent Samuel Shaffer, "Nixon's performance was unmatched by anyone in the history of American politics in an off-year election."

Everywhere Nixon asked the voters to give President Eisenhower a Congress which would carry out his policies. The President, he pointed out, had brought "peace to the world for the first time in fifteen years," had re-established "standards of honesty, loyalty, and integrity in our national government which were at an all-time low twenty months ago," and had instituted "economic policies which have brought America its best peacetime year in history." Against this he placed the Trumanesque policies which "over a period of twenty years resulted in either hard times or war." Electing Democrats would mean sending men to Congress who favored a return to the "foreign policy which resulted in the loss of 600 million people to the Communists in seven years," and to "policies which would mean higher spending, higher taxes, and controls . . . an economic philosophy which was taking the United States down the road to socialism."

"Communism should not be a political issue," he remonstrated. "There is no difference between the loyalty of Democrats and Republicans. But some misguided officials of the previous Administration were blind or indifferent to the danger. They ignored the repeated warnings that [FBI director] J. Edgar Hoover and others including myself brought to them." Citing the Hiss Case, the Harry White Case, and the systematic theft of atomic secrets by Soviet spies, Nixon added, "But this Administration is cooperating with J. Edgar Hoover. We have fired the Communists and fellow travelers and security risks by the thousands: * I can assure you that no one in this Administration regards communism as a red herring."

Though Nixon ranged much of the country, his major efforts were concentrated to the west of the Mississippi. In California, where his successor in the Senate, Thomas Kuchel, was in very serious difficulties, the Republican victory was directly attributable to Nixon's efforts. In the House elections the expected slaughter never developed. Despite the normal off-year trend against the party in power, the Republicans held their own, losing one seat and picking up another in the Mid- and Far West. In Oregon the Republicans lost a Senate seat, but by a microscopic margin. In the East, where Nixon merely did token campaigning, the losses were substantial—and in cases such as New York and Massachusetts,

---

* A wire-service report of a speech in which Nixon had made this statement eliminated "and fellow travelers and security risks"—giving the impression that Nixon had claimed that "thousands" of Communists had been fired. Democratic National Chairman Stephen Mitchell immediately accused Nixon of lying. Fortunately there was a tape recording of the speech, but Mitchell continued to use the "abridged" quotation in his attacks on Nixon. The figures at the time were: 2427 employees fired in all three categories—of which 383 had clearly subversive records.

directly traceable to resentment over the treatment of Mc-
Carthy.

Nixon's campaign tour served another, and vital, purpose.
His hard-hitting tactics brought the torpid Republican organization back to life. "I don't know whether Dick is changing any votes," a syndicated columnist told a high-ranking
Republican official during the campaign, "but he certainly is
a hero to the party organizations." From the precinct level to
the Congress, from the National Committee to the White
House, there were strong expressions of gratitude for his
work in the 1954 by-elections. Nixon was, in effect, the
cement which held together the left and right wings of the
Republican Party.

The highest compliment came from the Democrats. The
great sweep they had hoped for never materialized, though
they captured control of the Congress. And their bitterness
was great. "So far as we're concerned," said Speaker Sam
Rayburn, "his name is mud." Democratic strategists branded
Nixon Political Enemy Number 1, and Adlai Stevenson
accused him of perpetrating "McCarthyism in a white collar."
A freshman Democrat, Representative Harris B. McDowell,
shouted at a party function: "It's open season on the Vice
President." And open season it was, with the buckshot flying
in every direction—to the extent that President Eisenhower
took the opportunity at a press conference of reasserting his
trust in the Vice President.

When the Eighty-fourth Congress convened in January
1955, *U.S. News & World Report* told its readers:

> The man at the helm of the Republican Party, busily shap-
> ing policy and strategy for the 1956 Presidential contest, now
> turns out to be Vice President Richard M. Nixon. President
> Eisenhower wants it that way. In effect, he has made Mr.
> Nixon deputy leader of the party, virtually in charge of oper-
> ations . . . [This has] developed since the 1954 election
> . . . [a result of] a newer, closer bond between President
> and Vice President.

"The believing mind reaches its perihelion in the so-called liberals," Henry L. Mencken once wrote. "They believe in each and every quack who sets up his booth on the fair grounds, including the Communists. The Communists have some talents too, but they always fall short of believing in the liberals." Mencken linked this epigram to two syllogisms beloved of the "believing mind": "If you are against labor racketeers, then you are against the working man. If you are against demagogues, then you are against democracy." He might have added: "If you are against the Communists, then you are against the Bill of Rights."

Mencken never met Nixon, and it may be presumed that he would not have liked him. For Mencken was an earnest man who suspected in others what he considered a weakness in himself. But he would have understood Nixon—and paid grudging tribute to the rigorous single standard of political morality which Nixon applies. (He would have watched with glee the discomfiture of some Republicans who, having joined Nixon in the excoriation of Democrat Boyle, were caught short when Nixon called for the resignation of Republican Gabrielson.) He would have laughed at the passion which the troglodyte liberals expend in their dislike of Nixon. He would have recognized the genesis of this dislike, for Nixon is hated most by those who most hate themselves. And he would have seen in both the substance and the style of their outcries against Nixon what, in another context, he described as the "traditional Democratic method" of "howls, bellowings, and charges of fraud."

Richard Nixon is a political figure who has consistently neutralized efforts of friends and foe to mold him to a form alien to his own nature. From time to time the left and the right have attempted to recreate him in their own image. Having failed, they have ascribed their failure to a flaw in Nixon's character, to "opportunism," to a dozen other possible causes. The case against Nixon therefore becomes the case for him:

He exposed Alger Hiss, putting a "generation on trial," and thereby forcing the "believing mind" to question the unblemished purity of the New-Fair Deal. The pious claim that the non-Communist left was the most effective opponent of communism collapsed during the Hiss Case, creating an unbearable crisis in the "believing mind" which resolved itself, understandably enough, in a total rejection of anti-communism and the total acceptance of a curious body of anti-anti-Communist doctrine. There is nothing which is more embarrassing to a man with intellectual pride, particularly when he is arrogant in that respect, than to be proved wrong on any subject. Nixon was in the awkward position of having to prove virtually the entire press corps wrong on two great issues in which they had all gone on the record. The first was the Hiss Case, the second was the fund.

He displayed a direct, undramatic, and unfashionable love of country—subjecting all action to the simple criterion: "What's best for America?" But he would not accept as an article of faith the "believing" slogan, "What's bad for General Motors is good for America." He supported the United Nations, but he would not compromise that support—or his deep-rooted patriotism—by subscribing to the ritualistic belief in a super-mechanistic world state. Nor would he pay lip service to the tenet that any criticism of the UN was a crime against humanity. An internationalist in the sense that he saw

America's future and safety linked to the rest of the world, he nevertheless leaned to an older American dependence on temporary alliances for temporary purposes rather than "permanent" Holy Alliances.

He held the concept of an American society governed wherever possible by the free interplay of free forces—with government a mediator and not a partisan for or against labor, for or against industry, for or against South, North, East, or West. He respected the Bill of Rights as an instrument of the public weal, not as the fulcrum on which the lever of subversion could topple the Constitution.

He saw the future as a function of the past, the present as a function of both. "The American Revolution," he once said, "grew out of the English past. It was a logical progression. The French and Russian Revolutions tried to wipe the slate clean of the past—and they resulted in terror, universal dissension, and the total destruction of the ideals which gave them birth." But seeing tradition as a modifying factor, he could not accept any theory of dialectical inevitability. The New Deal had established certain patterns in American life, but he could not bow to the belief that all of these patterns were immutable, eternal, and irrevocable precursors of the regimented society sought by socialist theorists and activists.

This was the source of the body of ideas which sustained his political acts. But what frustrated the "believing mind" most thoroughly was Nixon's divorcement from any doctrinaire espousal. For politics, as well as economics, is a free interplay, and the man who holds cataleptically to doctrine ends up in the ADA, the Liberty League, or a mental ward. If war is the logical extension of diplomacy, accommodation is the logical concomitant of politics. The American climate deals unkindly with the Calhouns, the Bryans, and the La-Follettes. It is beneficent to the Lincolns who hold fast to principle but bend on specifics.

From his political beginnings Nixon has been deeply aware that most ideological labels are meaningless in the United

States. Shortly after he received the support of the Committee
of One Hundred, he wrote revealingly to Roy Day, one of his
sponsors. Under date of 4 December 1945, Nixon said, "Mr.
Voorhis' 'conservative' record must be blasted. But my main
efforts are being directed toward building up a positive,
progressive group of speeches which tell what we want to
do." He knew then that by the accepted labels of our time
Voorhis was not the "conservative" he posed as in California's
Twelfth District—though he himself was truly progressive.

Years later Nixon said in private conversation, "Liberal
and conservative are dirty words or compliments depending
on where you sit. Basically the liberals have no body of
thought—they just have a bunch of issues for which they
fight. That's why the CIO and the ADA can compile a list
of a congressman's votes and then tell you, 'See, this makes him
a liberal.' And then they have to duck because the most consistent 'liberal' by the standards they've set up turns out to be
a man like Vito Marcantonio. Then they have to suppress
some of my record on foreign aid and rent control and civil
liberties because I'd look too good by their own standards—
and after all, in their book, I'm the 'black reactionary' who
smeared Alger Hiss and made so much trouble for Mr. Truman."

The issues, as he recognized, were not the test. The touch-
stone was a man's approach to the issues. On the political
scene, for example, there was hardly a man who did not say
he was against communism—and in Congress the votes on
Communist control measures were well-nigh unanimous. But
the measure of a congressman's anti-communism was not his
votes on legislation, for the "believing mind" could go along
there even as it swallowed Senator Herbert Lehman's amendment to the Communist Control Act which created concen-
tration camps "in time of war." The disingenuous *reductio ad
absurdum* which made of the Communist problem a police
matter, limited to the catching of spies, was not for Nixon—
and it was here that he came into conflict with the non-Com-

munist left. In *The Faith of an Anti-Communist*, published
in *The Saturday Review of Literature* Nixon wrote:

> Communism is evil because it denies God and deifies man.
> "Man without God is a beast" [Whittaker] Chambers says,
> "never more beastly than when he is most intelligent about
> his beastliness." But evil though it is, communism has a tre-
> mendously malignant and potent appeal all over the world
> and right here, in the United States. This, then, is the lesson
> for us—that men become Communists out of the best of mo-
> tives and some of them cease to be Communists for the same
> motives once they learn that those who accept the pernicious
> doctrine of the end justifying the means will inevitably find
> that the means become the end. [We need] a counterfaith to
> combat the Communist idea—a faith based not on materialism
> but on a recognition of God. "Political freedom as the West-
> ern world knows it," Chambers says, "is only a political read-
> ing of the Bible."

There is a "believing mind" of the right as well—and when
the voice of the turtle and the "spirit of Geneva" were abroad
in the land, it attacked Nixon for speaking hopefully of peace.
The theory was proposed that he had "sold out" by putting
aside his anti-Communist principles in order to maintain
a cozy relationship with President Eisenhower. This, had it
been so, would have been no crime in practical politics, for
even so firm an opponent of some Administration policies as
Senator John W. Bricker could forget differences and an-
nounce himself for the "favorite son" sweepstakes as an Eisenhower man. What Nixon's critics forgot was this: In defending the "summit conference," and the sincere but abortive
attempt to seek decency in the Russians, he had circumscribed
his optimism by criteria which did no violence to his declared
principles of international relations:

> Is the cordiality of the Communists only calculated to get
> us to drop our guard so that they can attain more easily their
> objective of world conquest? [he asked in August, 1955].
> Here are some steps which the Communists can take to prove

that they honestly want to live in peace with the rest of the world:

Agree to free elections and the unification of Germany.

Withdraw Chinese Communist troops from North Korea and agree to free elections and unification.

Agree to the President's aerial inspection plan and thereby pave the way for disarmament.

Dismantle the barbed wire, the land mines, the watch towers, the machine guns of the Iron Curtain which divides the peoples of Europe.

Give freedom to the satellite countries.

Curtail the activities of Moscow-controlled Communist organizations in free nations.

What they do on these basic issues will determine whether there is a real thaw in the cold war, or just a brief warm spell before another big freeze. Affability can be simulated, and cordiality can be turned on and off like a faucet. Hard deeds are what the world wants to see.

These were words of challenge and hope—words which the Voice of America might have broadcast to the enslaved nations of the world. They were the practical application of other words, said by Woodrow Wilson and frequently quoted by Nixon: "A patriotic American is never so proud of the great flag under which he lives as when it comes to mean to other people as well as to himself a symbol of hope and liberty." Here was the fundamental motivation for the foreign aid which Nixon had so long and so actively espoused.

Again he confounded the "believing minds" of right and left—the shouters for all-out Federal subsidy of education and those whose fear of Federal encroachment blinded them to the grim needs of teachers and students. As Nixon saw it, the problem transcended rigid formulations. The purchasing power of industrial workers had more than doubled since the turn of the century; for teachers it had declined one per cent. Could the Federal government sit by, even though the states could, but would not, assume the financial responsibility, when schools and teachers were in such desperate shortage? Nixon raised this question at the White House Conference on Education. Education was no longer the luxury of a conscientious society, he said. In the growing technology of defense it was ineradicably linked to the national security, for without scientists and technicians the nation would perish. And he added:

> I think we should recognize at the outset that some Federal activity and responsibility is inevitable and necessary in the field of education. But we should have these caveats in mind . . . We must remember that we want our education to be free, and that freedom and Federal control are incompatible. There is no greater power that a government could exercise over a people than to be able to dictate what the young should learn. Our whole Constitutional system is based on the principle that diffusion of power is the best answer to tyranny and the best guarantee of freedom . . .
>
> Education to be great must be free. This means studying and discussing ideas we don't like as well as those we do. In this connection, it has been unfortunate that at a time when we are properly denying Communist Party members the right to teach in our schools, we have a tendency to go to the extreme of denying to our students the opportunity of learning about communism . . . Teaching students to be Communists is one thing. Teaching students about communism is another . . . We must never forget that the best answer to a false idea is not ignorance but the truth.

Here, as in all he did and all he believed, there was a confluence of the theoretical and the practical. The current of the merged streams bore his political boat. In the ten years of his public life it had carried him through the shoals of dissension and distortion and along the smooth waters of hope and achievement. There had been times of great discouragement, when he had envied those who drift in the backwaters. At such times he told friends, "After this, no more. No more campaigns, no more speeches, no more battles." But he did not change his course, for Nixon is first and foremost a political man.

On the eve of 1956 he could look back on ten years of dramatic rise. History and his own capabilities had catapulted him into high office. History and his own capabilities had made that office the second most important in the nation. From the "greenest congressman" he had become a Vice President unique in the life span of the Republic. Ahead was a year of decision, of sober surmise. On the third day of January the sound of Nixon's gavel echoed in the Senate chamber against a clamor of many voices. Some were friendly, some were not. For them all he had a felt but unspoken answer—a line of T. S. Eliot's poetry:

"For us, there is only the trying. The rest is not our business."